Through

MW01489218

I

Gave Birth

To

An Angel

Debbie Miller

Published by Ezekiel Publishing
www.ezekielpublishing.com
252 Hind Street
Tonawanda, New York, 14150

Cover design by Dugan Design Group
Interior design by Bethany Press International
Printed by Bethany Press International

ISBN: 978-0-578-09505-9

Dedication

This book is dedicated to all parents who have ever had a miscarriage, a stillborn, or lost a child in any way; and to anyone who ever knew someone who did but didn't know the right words to say to them; and to our son Michael Steven Miller, who was born (stillborn)
March 21, 1990.

Special Thanks

Special thanks to my loving husband, Steve,
who never gave up on me and gave me
the courage to face each day.
Also special thanks to my dear friend Sue,
who saw my life as a living testimony for Jesus.
But most of all, thank you, Jesus, for
your great Love and for being with me
through some of the hardest times in my life!

Foreword

Many people write books and tell their story of one kind or another, but very few people tell the whole brutal truth. Debbie Miller is an exception. She has told her story—the story of her son Michael who died in her womb. She has beared her soul. She has testified to her faith, but she has also told her moments of wrestling with unbelief. It is not a beautiful story. It is a story of pain...and blood...and great loss. But she has been honest. She has told the truth, and as a result, thousands and thousands of women (and men) will take courage and have the faith to live through their ordeal of suffering, pain and deep loss. By the time I finished her book, it was strange, but I never felt like Michael was gone. You feel his unborn presence, you realize he is still alive in Debbie's words of love...and you know she and her son will be united on that grand and glorious morning when we shall all be alive together...happy forevermore! In spite of all her pain, her wrestling with the powers of hell, Debbie ends up healed...and in victory. That makes her story even more of a miracle. She will not go through life with her head down; she will skip through the rest of her life with a song of joy, with the eye of faith, seeing her Michael around the throne of God.

Get Debbie's book and give it to one who has suffered the loss of a child, either before or after birth. You will do them a great favor and they will love you for your love and concern for them.

Debbie, thank you for a masterpiece!

Dr. Charles Green
President, Harvest Ministries to the World, Inc.
P. O. Box 293658
Lewisville, TX 75029

Read The Story,
Experience The Journey

There are some books that teach, others inspire, others speak truth. Seldom is there a book which teaches, inspires and shares the ultimate truth of He who is the truth. "Through A Mother's Eyes, I Gave Birth To An Angel" is that rare kind of a book.

Author Debbie Miller uses this manuscript to teach us how endure the most difficult of circumstances and come to the realization that no matter how devastating the things that we face in life, they can be used by God to help us to discover the real purposes of God for our lives. As we take this difficult journey with the author, we are inspired by her responses to circumstances which would have totally destroyed most people. Debbie truly inspires us. But most of all, she brings us to the ultimate truth of the person of Jesus Christ who can meet us at our lowest point and bring us to fulfillment and purpose.

So, I urge you to take this journey with Debbie. I did, and it became to me an experience that I will never forget. I walked with her as she faced the death of her special child and as she described the pain and suffering and fear that accompanied unbelievable health problems. She described them with such passion that I felt that I was laying on that hospital bed myself asking God if I would survive. I did take that journey with her, and it was a dramatic experience.

But most of all, she inspired me. She will also inspire you. You will feel the emotion of death being replaced with life, and with sickness being replaced with health.

So, join me in taking the journey. Discover the little angel and walk with Debbie into the ultimate victory of knowing Jesus. As you take the journey, you will cry and shed tears, you will wonder if she and you will survive, and you will stand at the end of the tunnel and find the ultimate victory that we always find in Christ.

Pastor Tommy Reid
The Tabernacle, Orchard Park, NY

Introduction

People say to me, "It can't happen! You can't give birth to an angel!" After you read this book, you decide. As for me...I already know. I gave birth to a little angel!

I'm no one special. But as for my son Michael, he must be. I know there are those of you reading this now who want answers. I don't have all the answers for you—I still don't have all my answers! I just pray that as you begin to read this book, you begin to heal! Yes...you too were blessed to know a little angel. For isn't that what parents call their little children...little angels? Our little ones will always be in our hearts! The Lord just needed our little angels more than we did, for reasons that we cannot at this time understand. But one day we will ...

Chapter 1

On July 27, 1985, I married the man of my dreams! Most girls dream of that perfect wedding, and I was no different. As I stood in the back of the church that hot summer day in Georgia, my mind began to wander. I couldn't believe how much my life had changed in less than a year. I ran my hand slightly down the front of my dress to my rounded belly. I was five months pregnant with my first child. I was built slender except for my belly, which looked like it had a soccer ball stuck up under my dress. I chuckled to myself at the thought of how my body was changing. I could feel the baby moving around inside of me a lot lately. Today, however, the baby seemed to be more active than usual. I guess we were both very nervous!

I was twenty-five years old and about to change my life forever. I had thought that my life was not worth anything. Now something was happening inside me. I couldn't explain it, but for the first time in my life I was feeling like I belonged somewhere and to someone! I had a hard life growing up, and I really thought I didn't deserve to be this happy. All I truly cared about at that moment was the baby and my husband, Steve. I had never felt this way about anyone before. They meant the whole world to me, and I was determined to be the best mom and wife that I could be for them. I had made a lot of mistakes in my life and I was determined to put it all behind me. Steve brought me so much happiness! He believed in me, and now for the first time in my life, I was beginning to believe in myself! As I looked down at my stomach, I began to smile. "This is the happiest day of my life, and I am the luckiest woman I know," I said to myself. "Everything from here on in my life is going to be perfect!"

Steve and I both knew how wrong it was to have sex before marriage. But we cared deeply for each other, so we made excuses and one thing led to another. You always think it will never happen to you—that you would never get pregnant. Then all of a sudden reality hits you in the face. I was on birth control while we were dating. This pregnancy had not been planned, it just happened. I had been born to an unwed mother and had never gotten to know my father growing up. I wanted more than that for my child! Before we knew it, Steve and I had to make some very important decisions in our lives. It was time to face reality! At the time, we had one thing going for us: we were beginning to fall in love with each other. I don't know what would have happened if there had been no love there.

We both knew that this baby needed both of us—a mother and a father. We were determined to raise it in a good home filled with lots of love. As I look back now, I know that the Lord was already controlling our lives and our destiny. Even if we had forgotten Him and sinned, He never forgot us! I had been saved as a little girl but had drifted away from the Lord. Steve had been raised Amish and in a good Christian home, but he too had forsaken the Lord, just like me. We had given in too easily to the temptations of this world. But God had a plan, and He had brought us together!

Was I ready for this? Ready or not, it was really happening to me! I knew Steve would make a great dad because he was such a good man! But I wasn't sure what type of mother I would be. What did I have to offer this new little one? I truly didn't feel that I had anything to give this baby but my love, and I wasn't sure if that would be enough. Steve was so excited over this baby, and it wasn't even born yet. I hoped so much that the baby might be a boy. Steve always loved the outdoors—loved things like hunting and fishing. If this was a boy, Steve could do so many things with him. Then I thought to myself what fun I could have if it was a little girl. I could play dress-up with my own real-live baby doll.

It's funny how you think of things right before you are about to walk down the aisle to get married. I knew I had made the right decision to to marry Steve! My mind was racing so fast that I couldn't even keep up with it. I was thinking about the past, the present and about what might happen in the future. All at once I stopped and looked up at the front of the church and saw Steve. I could tell that he was as nervous as I was. It actually made me feel much better to see him that way. I knew in my heart that after today I would never be the same again. I was ready; I needed Steve in my life! I was ready to have my own family. So...I became Mrs. Steve Miller that day. I was so proud to be his wife and to carry his child. I was so happy! I now had someone to share the rest of my life with and I would never feel alone again!

Chapter 2

Who writes the books on pregnancy? Can anyone really answer me that question? By my ninth month I could barely move around. My walk became a waddle, and I couldn't see my feet anymore! I was eating everything in sight, and it showed. I no longer had that skinny figure I had been known for; now all I felt was fat! The worst thing of all was it seemed like I spent all my time either eating or sick in the bathroom. This wasn't what I thought pregnancy would be like. The Hollywood version looked much better. I had read all kind of books on the subject of being pregnant, but they didn't seem to mention all this in full detail. I was always tired; I couldn't even get comfortable lying down to sleep anymore.

I began to have false contractions more frequently near my due date. I had convinced myself that after this baby was born, there would be no more children. Why did women go through this? I couldn't believe all the changes that a woman's body had to go through just to have a baby. I had gained a lot of weight and I thought I would be fat forever. I must have whined a lot to Steve, but he never complained. He did the best he could to help me relax and to cheer me up. Steve always seemed to be there with a caring smile and a gentle hug to tell me that everything would be all right. His love gave me so much strength! It didn't even seem to bother him that I looked like a big fat cow. At least, that is what I thought I looked like.

Well, my due date came and went, and I was still pregnant! "Can it be that I will never have this child!" I would say those words over and over again to myself till it sounded like a broken record. The excitement of being pregnant was now gone! The doctors told me not to worry—that everything was fine. Fine? I wasn't fine! I wanted this baby out! My due date, I had been told, was around Thanksgiving, and here it was almost Christmas. The doctors told me that it was perfectly normal for a woman to go a little bit over her due date with her first child. Is this what they called "a little bit over"? I had gone weeks over, not days. It was almost Christmas and I still had all my Christmas shopping to do. What was I going to do?

Finally the day arrived! I began to have hard contractions early one morning. I called my doctor, who told me to come in to the office once they opened that morning. I looked at the clock and realized I still had a whole hour till anyone would be there. I paced the floor of my mobile home, waiting for every minute to go by. The clock moved very slowly. That had to be one of the longest mornings I have ever experienced. Once I was in his office, he examined me and told me that I was in the first stages of labor and that I was almost dilated. Almost, was he kidding? I was in pain! First stages? That was the last thing I wanted to hear. How many more stages did I have to go? The big question was, Could I really go through all of this? And what if I changed my mind? Boy, was that a silly question to even think!

My doctor told me that I needed to go over to the hospital, where they could monitor me. He told me that I needed to walk around there, that it would help me to dilate faster. My mom took me over to the hospital and got me checked in to the labor-and-delivery room. This baby would be her first grandchild and she was so excited! I was the only one not feeling all the excitement at that very moment. I began to walk the halls of the hospital—I walked and I walked—which is not the easiest thing to do when you are having hard contractions and in pain!

My mom walked with me for several hours, then Steve came and relieved her. I had called Steve earlier in the day and told him just to keep working, that the doctor had said this delivery could take hours. *What?* I couldn't believe what I was hearing. All I could do was try to hold back the tears while I was talking to Steve. I think Steve and Mom had the easiest job; all they had to do was walk with me. I don't know how I would have made it if my mom wouldn't have been there for me. I had heard stories of women having babies so easily—they just went into the hospital and minutes later they had a baby. And what about those women who take nothing for their pain during childbirth? Are they nuts? I was begging for something for the pain, but they told me I needed to be more dilated. At that time, nothing made any sense to me.

What had seemed to take forever at the time now seems to have happened so fast! About thirty-two hours after checking into the hospital, we brought a beautiful little girl into the world. The look on Steve's face will be with me forever! He was so proud of her! It didn't even seem to matter to him that the baby was a girl instead of a boy. We named her Jessica Lynn Miller. She was born December 19, 1985, at 12:56 in the afternoon. As I looked at her little fingers and toes, all I could feel was pure joy. I felt no pain from the childbirth at all now. It was like it had all vanished into thin air. This tiny life had brought peace all over me! This little one now needed me as much as I needed her. I grabbed Steve's hand and started crying. Now I was a mom; now we were a family. For the first time, I felt like I understood the real meaning of life.

Chapter 3

Nothing you read about can prepare you for motherhood; you have to live through it. Jessica had colic! I don't remember who cried more, her or me. From the time the sun went down till the time the sun came up, she cried! Praise God that only lasted the first few months of her life. I watched my little baby begin to grow and turn into a toddler. I never realized that there was so much responsibility in raising a child. The television shows I had watched sure made it seem easy. Boy, were they wrong! Steve and I had both decided we didn't want to have any more children. Or at least, that was what we had thought.

As Jessica grew older, I felt myself longing to have another baby. Had I forgotten what it was like to be pregnant? I can't put into words how much I wanted another child. Everywhere I went, it seemed like someone had a little baby and I wanted to hold them. I would try to tell Steve stories about why we should have another baby. But he would just shake his head and tell me that one was quite enough. I didn't want Jessica to grow up as an only child. She needed to have a brother or sister to play with and take care of. I wanted her to have the family I never had! All I thought about was having another baby. So I started praying that I would get pregnant.There is a reason people say be careful what you ask for.

When Jessica was about fifteen months old, I became pregnant. Steve was not very thrilled over the idea. I was—until I began to get morning sickness nonstop. How could I have forgotten this sick feeling? What had I been thinking? I was sick every morning and every night. The thought of food made me sick, smelling certain smells made me sick. I was a total mess! Then I began to spot blood. At first just a little bit, then it got heavier. I had done the same thing with Jessica in the early stages of pregnancy, so I wasn't too worried. After a few days, I thought it would stop. But it never did!

Soon I began to worry about all the bleeding. I called my doctor, and he told me to stay off my feet in order for the bleeding to stop and that I needed to have complete bed rest for a while. Was he kidding me? I had an active toddler who wouldn't sit still, and my doctor wanted me to go to bed. I didn't see any way that could happen. Both our parents lived out of state, and I had no one to help me. Steve couldn't stay home with me and miss work; we needed the money. What was I suppose to do? I did the best I could each day to get rest, considering all I had to keep up with.Then it happened: I went into the bathroom one evening and discovered that I was bleeding even more heavily. I started developing terrible cramps in my lower stomach. I was afraid because I didn't know what was happening to me. I yelled for Steve, and soon we were on our way to the hospital. Once there, the nurses in the labor room called my doctor. One of the nurses told me I would need to stay overnight in the hospital— that I was trying to miscarry. Trying to miscarry? How was I trying to do that? Why was this happening to me? My world was being turned upside down!

That evening in the hospital, I miscarried, or so it's called. The doctor told me later that I had lost part of the baby or babies at home and the rest there in the hospital. He even told me that the way it looked, I could have been pregnant with twins. My heart felt so cold and empty! Why hadn't I tried harder to keep this baby? I blamed myself for everything that had happened. I was grieving for my baby, or babies. I didn't even know if it was a boy or girl, one or even two babies; I just knew that my heart missed my baby! People said things to me like, "You can try again. Maybe something was wrong with it."

And of course my favorite: "It's better this way." Better? Better for who?

No matter what anyone said to me, they couldn't take away my pain. That was my baby, a part of me, and now he or she was gone forever! I just couldn't pretend it didn't happen. It was a human life, and I was grieving for it! Didn't anyone understand? Even Steve didn't seem to understand how I felt. I felt so alone, so lost. I had for a brief moment this little life inside of me, and now in a blink of an eye, it was gone! Why did people act like it wasn't anything important?

This baby was a part of me! How could I make anyone understand? Even though I hadn't held this baby or even seen his or her face, it had still been my child. When a woman finds out she is pregnant, it is a very special moment in her life. Words can't explain what it is like to know that there is a little life inside of you growing every day. You even find yourself talking to the baby. The bond between a mother and her unborn child is like no other in this world! But now my baby was gone. I had so many questions, like, *Where is my baby now? Was it a boy or girl? Was it really twins? Did they throw him or her away? What did they do with my baby?*

When I started thinking of all of these things, it made me sick! I felt so helpless. Why did this happen to us? Where could I turn to for answers? Who really could understand this loss that I felt? At that moment, I thought I was the only one who had ever been through this. To this day I still think of this baby. I often wonder if it really was twins. When I hear that someone has had a miscarriage, it rips at my heart and I remember the pain I felt. You never truly forget what it feels like to lose a child! I thought to myself, *This is what they call a miscarriage? The losing of a baby?* The word just didn't seem to fit! My baby was a life, a part of me. To me, this is not called a miscarriage...it's called a *baby*! How can a person ever get over this loss? Who truly cares when you miscarry?

Chapter 4

They say time heals all wounds. I guess that is true. After a period of time, I found myself wanting to be pregnant again. What was I thinking? Had I forgotten that I had just lost a baby? At the time, that didn't even seem to matter to me. I just knew my heart yearned to have another baby. Once you get that feeling, it is just hard to put it into words! Steve was not at all thrilled over this idea. He hated the thought of seeing me get hurt all over again. I was just starting to be happy, the way I had used to be. I kept telling him that things would be different with the next pregnancy. I think I tired to reassure myself, as well as Steve.

Steve could tell how much I wanted another child. He said he would do anything to make me happy, and if it meant another child, then he would agree to it. He knew how much having a family meant to me. After waiting what seemed to be forever, it happened. I became pregnant! We had almost given up hope that I would ever get pregnant again. This time I would watch everything I did. I was determined to keep this baby. Steve didn't get as excited with this baby at first, because he was afraid something might happen during the pregnancy. Deep down I was afraid too, but I tried not to show it. I was determined to make it through this pregnancy!

Soon I began to bleed just like before. I was so afraid to see this happening again. But before I knew it, much to my surprise the bleeding stopped. As the months went by, Steve began to get excited over this pregnancy too! All in all, I had a pretty good pregnancy with very few problems. I didn't even seem to care this time about putting on weight! I worked right up until my due date running a nursery in a health club. I was having so much fun being pregnant! I came to find out that no two pregnancies are the same. Steve and I didn't care if this baby was a boy or girl. What mattered the most to both of us was that we had a healthy baby!

Soon my delivery date came, and I began to have false contractions just like when I was pregnant with Jessica. There is nothing worse than having hard contractions that last for a long time and going to the hospital just to find out that they are not the real thing. It seemed like once I was in the hospital and hooked up to their monitors, my contractions would just stop! I went to the hospital so many times that I began to know the nurses by name. One night after being at the hospital and finding out my pain was only a false contraction again, I made up my mind; I wasn't going back to the hospital until I saw or felt the baby's head.

I woke up one morning around two o'clock with heavy cramps in my lower stomach and in my back. *Not again,* I thought to myself. How much pain can a person take? I got up out of bed and began to pace the floor. I got in and out of warm showers (I had been told that warm showers would help when having contractions). I did everything I could think of to help ease the pain. Steve just slept through it all. After several long hours of contractions, I began to bleed. Now I was afraid something was wrong with the baby. I couldn't bear the thought of losing another child! My mind began to race with questions. *Have I waited too long? Should I have gone to the hospital? What if something is wrong with the baby?* So many things were racing through my mind and I was beginning to panic!

I woke Steve up right away and told him that I needed to go to the hospital. He was still in a daze when I told him that I was bleeding. When he heard those words, he jumped out of our bed like someone had hit him. Steve called my doctor, and the doctor said that he would meet us at the hospital. He told us not to worry, that it was time for the baby. What did he mean, time for the baby? What did he mean, not to worry? Was he kidding? I had absolutely no idea what was happening. All I knew was I was now bleeding and it was getting heavier! This was not the way I had planned things. Why couldn't I be like an average pregnant woman and have a baby with no problem? Why did I have to make everything so hard? Why was I bleeding so much? I thought to myself, *This can't be normal!*

Once at the hospital, the nurses reassured me that everything was fine. They said that I was just dilating very quickly. By now I was having really hard contractions. Steve stayed with me through it all, as always. I don't think I could have made it through any of this without him by my side! He is always there for me when I need him the most! Four hours after entering the hospital, we delivered another bouncing baby girl into the world. We named her Jennifer Kay. She was so tiny when she was born, compared to Jessica. The first thing I did was look at her tiny fingers and toes and count them. Don't ask me why— some mothers just do that! She was so perfect! Steve and I both were so happy. We now had two beautiful girls, and Jessica was now a big sister.

Chapter 5

There I was, a mother of two little girls—a three-year-old and a newborn. Boy, was I busy! Like Jessica, Jennifer had colic. I was up all night with her. Then it happened. I got the baby blues. I had heard stories of women getting depressed after having a baby, but I didn't believe it could happen to me. Boy, was I wrong! I was so depressed over things. I didn't like the way I looked. I didn't like where we lived. You might say I just wasn't happy about anything! If you even looked at me, I would either cry or snap at you. I just could not control my emotions, no matter how hard I tried. I even began to have trouble sleeping, and eating seemed to be very hard for me to do.

I soon began to get very homesick for our family and friends who lived in Ohio. We were still living in Georgia at the time, and everyone dear to me just seemed very far away. I missed the place where we were raised, the place I had always called home. I began to feel like I was losing everything and everyone in my life. I felt so lost and all alone! I wanted to go home, back to Ohio. It was hard for me to tell Steve that I wanted to leave Georgia. We both had come to love it so much. Now my heart just didn't feel at home here anymore.

I began to whine to Steve that I wanted us to move back to Ohio. He had to have thought his wife was nuts. I had always told him that we should never move back to Ohio, and here I was telling him I wanted to move back. Steve tried so hard to make me forget all my worries, but nothing he said could make me feel better. He soon began to realize that I really wasn't happy living so far away from our families. When Jennifer was six weeks old, we packed up everything we owned and moved back to Ohio. It was a big move for us with two little ones!

Steve didn't have a job waiting in Ohio and we didn't know where we would live. Yet we were on our way. Somehow we would make it; we always seemed to make it through anything! We stayed with my mom for a period of time and soon we found a house. Steve was able to get his old job back where he had worked when we first met. Everything seemed to be falling into place. I was feeling much better and seemed to be coming out of the baby blues stages. Being a mother of two little girls was beginning to be a lot of fun! Things were going so perfect for us, or so I thought.

Soon I started getting sick like I had the flu. I tried to ignore it, I thought it was just a bug or something I ate. Then one morning I woke up with a terrible toothache. Steve joked with me about having a toothache. I think he thought I was kidding around. For some weird reason every time I got pregnant, I always got a toothache! I knew I couldn't be pregnant; Jennifer was only ten weeks old and I was breast-feeding her. Everyone knows you can't get pregnant when you breastfeed! At least that's what I had always been told. We both laughed at even the thought of me being pregnant; I hadn't even had a period. It was impossible—or was it?

My toothache kept hurting and getting worse and I was feeling more and more sick no matter what I tried to do or what pills I took. Finally I decided to go to a dentist. He told me that I had chipped a tooth and that it needed to be pulled. He also said that the tooth was infected, which was probably the reason I was so sick. So he pulled the tooth and gave me some pills for infection to take two times a day. I thought I would start feeling better in a couple of days, but I didn't. Another week went by, and I didn't seem to be getting any better. I was light-headed and sick to my stomach. I couldn't keep any food down.

I finally decided that I had better go to a doctor to see what was wrong with me. I had a complete physical and also some blood work done on me. I thought that my body was just tired and that I had caught a really bad flu. As I was getting dressed to leave, a nurse came into the room and told me that she needed to talk to me before I leave. She told me that they had run a pregnancy test as well as other tests on my blood. She then informed me that the pregnancy test had came back positive—that I was pregnant. She told me I was only a few weeks pregnant and that it would have never shown up on a urine test, only a blood test.

All of a sudden I just froze; those words hit me like a ton of bricks. *Oh my God,* I said to myself, *I am pregnant!* It wasn't a joke anymore and I wasn't laughing. The nurse told me I needed to stop breast-feeding Jennifer right away. I was in shock and so was Steve when I told him the news later that day. For whatever reason, Steve seemed to take this pregnancy much better than I did. I could barely handle these two little girls, and now another one was on its way. We didn't even plan this; it just happened! All I could do was cry. After a period of weeks the shock finally wore off and I began to get excited over this pregnancy. I just couldn't get over holding a little baby and knowing that I had one growing in my tummy at the same time.

Soon I began to bleed a little just like all of the other pregnancies. After several weeks of spotting, one morning it just up and stopped. I always worry about those first few months of being pregnant, since I would always bleed a little bit. I figured that if there was anything wrong with the pregnancy, it would show up then. I was feeling so good by now that it actually amazed me! My morning sickness didn't even last as long as it did with the other pregnancies. Maybe after so many pregnancies the morning sickness just goes away more quickly. I was home free with this pregnancy; the worst was behind me. I had made it through the first few months, and now nothing could go wrong!

Chapter 6

When I was five months pregnant, suddenly I began to bleed a little again. I called my doctor right away, I was so terrified! He told me not to worry, but to get off of my feet right away. I did exactly what I was told and after a couple of days the bleeding stopped. Before I knew it I was allowed to get back up. A few days later, I was in the kitchen cooking supper when I sneezed. Suddenly, I felt something trickle down my leg. As I looked down towards the floor, I saw blood running down my leg. When I tried to move, I got a terrible pain in my lower stomach, as if someone had hit me in my belly. *Oh God,* I thought, *not the baby. I'm only a few months pregnant.*

I somehow made it to the phone and called Steve at work. Before I knew it, he was home and we were heading straight to the hospital. All I kept thinking about was this baby. I knew that if he was born now, he wouldn't make it. Yes, somehow I knew it was a boy. It was just this feeling deep down inside of me. It's something I can't explain; I think some moms just know! I found myself praying to God for help that day, something that I hadn't done in a long time. It's funny how you can call out to God only when something is going wrong in your life. I didn't know what else to do; praying to God just seemed to be the only answer. I was so scared and so was Steve. I knew in my heart that I just couldn't make it through another miscarriage. *Why is this happening?* I kept asking myself over and over again in my mind. Once we were at the hospital, my doctor met us in the emergency room and then I was rushed upstairs to the Labor and Delivery Room.

Everyone was trying to be so nice to me, but I could tell by the look on their faces that they were worried too. The pain had stopped now and the bleeding had slowed down. The nurses could tell how worried I was and that I was listening to every word being said around me. They kept telling me that everything would be all right, and that I should just relax. Who were they kidding? How could I relax? I knew something was terribly wrong. I was told that they were going to keep me overnight so they could monitor me and the baby. Monitor us for what? I could not understand what was going on and I wanted answers.

My doctor quietly sat down next to me on the bed and told me that my body was trying to go into labor and have the baby. He told me it would probably happen that night. He also explained to me that the baby probably wouldn't make it because I wasn't far enough along for him to live. I couldn't believe what I was hearing. All of my pain had stopped, the contractions had stopped, and now my bleeding had stopped. I was feeling pretty good and wanted to go home. Now here I was, being told that I would lose my baby. Why was he telling me this? Nothing made any sense to me!

Later that same evening, I watched the baby's heartbeat on the monitor. The baby seemed to be doing just fine. Everything seemed to be so peaceful to me. I looked over at Steve, who had fallen asleep on the chair beside me. I couldn't believe all that I had put Steve through. All I wanted to do was to give him a son. All of this seemed like a bad dream and I was right in the middle of the whole thing! I did a lot of praying that night. I told God how much I wanted this baby. I just lay there in my hospital bed waiting for something to happen with my body, but it never did.

Soon morning came and I was still pregnant. My doctor couldn't believe that he hadn't been called in the night for me. All of my symptoms were gone! The baby was very active inside of me now and his heartbeat was normal. The doctor told me that he didn't see any reason why he should keep me and that I could go home. My younger sister was still worried about me and the baby so she called a specialist in a nearby town. He asked her if I could be brought to him after leaving the hospital so he could examine me. As soon as I was checked out of the hospital, I was on my way to see him. I was still feeling really good!

Once I got to the new doctor's office, they ran lots of tests. *Now maybe I will get some answers to what happened.* I was there for several hours before the doctor had me go back to his office for the results. By then I was so tired and I couldn't wait to go home. The doctor told me that some of my amniotic fluid had leaked out from around the baby but that it was only a small amount and I shouldn't worry about it. He told me that the baby had a strong heartbeat and seemed to be doing fine. The doctor then confirmed what I had already known in my heart—that we were going to have a boy!

Steve was so excited to hear the news that we were going to have a son. His smile was worth a thousand words to me! It's funny how I had felt all along it was a boy. The doctor told me I would need to go home and have total bed rest for a while and that he would monitor me very closely. He also said that I need-ed to come in every two weeks for a checkup. I was now consid-ered a high-risk pregnancy, whatever that meant. He reassured me that everything would be just fine. What a relief! Now maybe I could finally relax! I could feel the baby moving a lot inside of me. The worst was over now. *One day soon, we will laugh over this scare you gave us.*

Chapter 7

Being bedridden can get to a person after a period of time. I wanted to get up so badly I could taste it! I had always been very active in everything I did. It was so hard for me to lie there in bed and watch other people do my housework and cook my meals. But what choice did I have? After a long week of bed rest,the doctor said I could finally get up. I was feeling like my old self again. I was going to the doctor's office every two weeks, and both the baby and I were doing very well! I knew in my heart that before long this pregnancy would be over.

The baby was getting more and more active inside of me as I was getting closer to my due date. All of the problems with this pregnancy the past few months now just seemed like a bad dream. I was home free with this pregnancy—or so I thought. A few weeks before my due date, as I was planning Jennifer's first birthday party, I realized that the baby did not seem to be as active inside of me as usual. I had just been to the doctor the week before and was told that we were doing great, so I didn't try to think too much of the problem.

As the day went on, I kept feeling like I was getting the flu or some type of bug. My body just did not feel right; I felt strange! I reassured myself that it was because I was pregnant and near the due date. I shook off those feelings as much as I could and tried to keep myself busy. That night I felt so terrible, I could barely sleep. I tossed and turned in our bed till finally I got up and began to walk through the house. I noticed that my belly seemed to be dropping, which normally happens near a woman's due date, so I did not worry.

I went ahead and had Jennifer's party the next day and tried to keep my mind off of worrying about the pregnancy. By that evening, however, I noticed I wasn't getting any better and that the baby wasn't moving around as usual at all. That night I could not sleep again; I was up and down continually. I felt so sick to my stomach and I did not know why. I would look at my large belly in the mirror and try to reassure myself that everything was ok, but somehow I knew it wasn't. I knew it would not be long till I would hold my little baby in my arms. I finally decided to wake up Steve and tell him I wasn't feeling the best and that I was worried about the baby. He told me not to worry and suggested I call the doctor in the morning.

I called the doctor first thing the next morning and he also reassured me not to worry. He told me to eat something right away and to lie flat on my back for a while. He said it was common near a woman's due date for the baby to become less active. I trusted him, so I did just what he told me to do, but still the baby did not move! Again I called my doctor. I am sure I became a pest, but somehow I knew something was wrong. He again told me not to worry, but to be on the safe side I should come right in to his office and that he would check me. I called Steve at work, and the secretary told me he was working out of town. What was I going to do? What would I do with the girls?

The secretary could hear fear in my voice. She asked me what was wrong and I told her I needed to go to the doctor right away—that the baby didn't seem to be moving. She told me I shouldn't drive myself to the doctor's office, so she offered to take me there. I was glad because I didn't feel much like driving. I hung up with her and called my mom and Steve's mom. I tried not to sound like I was worried, but I know they could tell I was. Steve's mom said she would come and stay with the girls.

The drive to the doctor's office was a long one! There was a stillness in the air; neither one of us knew what to talk about. I don't think she knew what to say to me. And the truth is, I didn't know what to say to her either. All I could do was think about this baby. I kept putting my hand on my belly hoping to feel movement, but there was none. *He's sleeping,* I kept telling myself. *He is just like his dad, who can sleep through anything.* I tried the best I could to reassure myself that everything was all right. But did I really believe it? So many thoughts were running through my mind and I was fighting every one of them. I know I was very scared—for me and for the baby!

Once we got to the doctor's office, we had to sit in the waiting room for what seemed to be a long time. Then a nurse came in. She took me into a room and told me she needed to listen to the baby's heartbeat just to make sure everything was fine. This was usually standard procedure, so I wasn't worried. I lay back on the table and she began to try to listen to the baby's heartbeat using a stethoscope. All at once she looked at me, very puzzled. Next thing I knew she was telling me I needed to have an ultrasound done. Even then I didn't seem to worry, because I had had that procedure done to me before. The nurse told me they needed to make sure the baby was not in a stressful position. We both talked about our pregnancies and laughed at each other's stories. It really seemed to help relieve the tension! She made me feel very relaxed!

We were just talking while I was having the ultrasound done, when suddenly right in the middle of a sentence she just froze and looked up at me. Next thing I knew she was running out of the room in tears. I just lay there for a few minutes trying to figure out what happened. Then I leaned over and looked at the screen. Yep, there was my little boy, and it looked like he was sleeping. I moved my body forward to get a better look at the picture on the ultrasound monitor. The nurse had turned the monitor more her way before she left the room. *Where is she,* I thought. *What happened? What did she see that made her run out of the room crying?* I had to find out what had just happened.

Chapter 8

The nurse was gone a long time. I noticed my baby on the screen, but something was different. The baby wasn't moving! He just kept lying in the same position; he wasn't even moving a little bit. I began to move my belly with my hand to get him to move, but still nothing. "Come on, wake up!" I said jokingly, but still nothing happened. I looked at the screen in shock! What was happening? I began to move my belly harder. "Would you wake up!" I said, shouting to the baby in my belly as tears began to fill my eyes.

"You gotta move...you just gotta!" I started speaking loudly at the screen, but still nothing happened. The air in the room began to get very thick. I didn't know if I was going to pass out or throw up. The inside of my head began to spin out of control and I could feel my heart racing. I just lay back down looking helpless at my baby on the monitor. I kept hoping and praying to see any kind of movement, but none came. I felt a tear run down my face. I could feel myself becoming angry! *No, I thought to myself, everything is fine! My baby boy is fine; he's just sleeping!*

Looking back on it now, what seemed to take forever was probably just a few minutes. It seemed like time had stopped and was just standing still! Finally two doctors walked into the room. Neither of them said a word to me at first. They just walked over to the monitor, looked at the screen and pushed a few buttons. I lay there silently, watching them. I had no idea what was happening. My heart was beating so fast I thought it would pop! All at once one of the doctors looked at me and told me to get dressed. Then they both turned and walked out without saying another word to me. I reassured myself by thinking everything was okay and a mistake had been made. I just wanted to go home; I had had enough for one day!

A few minutes later, a nurse came into the room and asked me to follow her. She took me down a long dark hallway and into an office, where both of the doctors were waiting for me. I tried to look cheerful, but I had a terrible feeling deep inside of me. All I wanted to do was run out of that office and I didn't even know why! One of the doctors offered me a seat. The other asked me if I would like something to drink. They both tried to make me feel as comfortable as they could. *Why are they being so nice to me?* Then they both began talking to me very slowly. They told me how sorry they were. *Sorry? Sorry for what?* I thought to myself. Their eyes began to swell up with tears as they looked at me. I could tell they were having a hard time telling me something, but it wasn't make any sense!

They knew how much this pregnancy meant to me! Now here they were trying to tell me...that my baby was dead! I will never forget the sound of their voices and the word in my head echoing *"dead."* It cut me like a knife—a pain so deep, there are no words to describe it! As they were talking to me, their voices seemed to be getting farther and farther away. They kept asking me if I was all right? Were they kidding? I could hear every word they were saying, but it was if they were speaking to me down a long tunnel. Their words just seemed to be echoing in my head.

They said so many things to me that day, most of which I can't even remember. I was unable to even open my mouth and talk to them; all I could do was listen helplessly. In my head I was screaming for someone to help me! *There's been a terrible mistake!* I said to myself. *This can't be happening—someone do something! Please...please don't let my baby die! Someone, anyone...please help me!* But no one could hear my words. I couldn't speak no matter how hard I tried. My screams were only echoing in my head.

There is just no way that God would take my child. I had prayed for this baby for a long time. Didn't He hear my prayers? We didn't go to church anywhere or live a Christian life, but we weren't bad people! Why was God punishing us? There had to be a mistake! The doctors did the best they could to explain things to me and to comfort me for my loss. But what could anyone say to make me feel better? To make this pain go away? I felt no one had any idea what I was going through! And I really didn't know if I would even make it through this.

They told me that Steve had been called. That was the first I had even thought about Steve. My mind had raced to my own grief and my own pain. Now I wondered how Steve would take this. I was told that he would be there in about two hours or so to pick me up. When the secretary from where Steve worked (the one who had brought me to the doctor) found out that my baby was dead, she left the office crying. They said she had told them that she just couldn't face me. Those words didn't even seem to bother me. Now all I could do was think of Steve. How would he deal with the loss of his son? How could I face him? I kept feeling sick inside like I was going to throw up. What words could I say to him? I felt like my whole world had just been turned upside down. Why was this happening to us?

Chapter 9

The doctor's office called the local hospital to try to get me into the labor & delivery room as soon as possible. But of course the labor & delivery room was booked for the night. They told me there were no openings till early the next morning. The doctors both agreed that it would be best to wait till then—there was no choice. They told me I would be sent home for the night and that they would meet me there first thing in the morning. I was then told that I would have to go through normal childbirth to have this baby. They would induce my labor, and as quickly as they could, they would get the baby out. They made the soonest appointment they could to get me in the hospital. It would be the following morning at six o' clock. The rest of what they told me, I can't remember—it was all just to much for me to handle!

One of the doctors wanted to give me some type of pills to help me relax. I shook my head and told him I didn't need any. I was already numb now; there really weren't any feelings to worry about. Nothing seemed to hurt but my broken heart, and they couldn't give me a pill for that or even try to mend it. It had broken into pieces! I guess they did the best they could for me. What can you say to a person once you tell them their child is dead?

I went out into the waiting room to wait for Steve. I looked at the other pregnant women that were waiting for the doctor in the waiting room. Some were complaining to each other about their aches and pains. *That had once been me,* I thought to myself. Now I wished I had those pains! I didn't talk to anyone, I just kept to myself. I sat alone in a corner of the waiting room and just stared off into space. I couldn't even cry. Looking back now, I believe I was probably in shock. A nurse kept coming out and asking if she could get me anything. I would just shake my head and tell her no. How could I tell her that all I wanted was my baby?

What would I say to Steve when I saw him? Sorry just didn't seem to be the right word. He didn't deserve this! Steve had always been there for me; now I needed to be there for him. I kept telling myself to be strong, but I couldn't find any strength to grab hold of. How could I look into Steve's eyes and tell him that his only son was dead? Had the doctor's office already told him? And if they did, would he be upset with me? I began to blame myself for the death of our son. Thoughts that maybe I did something that caused this kept running through my head. All I had was time to think while I sat there waiting for Steve. I felt so alone, yet there were people all around me. My dream of the prefect family was falling apart!

Soon Steve came. He pulled up in his big work truck and opened the door for me. I had seen him pull in, so I went out to meet him. If he would have picked me up in his work truck before, being pregnant I would have yelled. It had been too hard for me to get in and out of, but now it didn't seem to matter. He asked if I was all right. What was I going to tell him—that I was falling apart inside? I looked out the window once I got in the truck and told him I was fine. What else could I say? I couldn't even look at him. I could feel pain in his voice when he talked to me. I really didn't say much to him all the way home. I don't think either one of us knew what to say.

Once we got home, I went right inside without saying a word. The house now felt cold and empty. I had never noticed that feeling before in our house. When the girls spotted me, Jessica came running. *Be strong,* I told myself. *Don't you dare cry in front of these little girls!* I tried to be my happy self, but everyone could tell I wasn't. Jessica kept asking me, "Are you all right, Mommy?" I had to tell her I was; I had no choice. The hardest thing for me, though, was when she asked me if she could feel the baby kick? She was so excited over this baby, and she loved to feel him kick her!

Every time Jessica would ask me about the baby, the words cut right to my heart. I knew she did not understand, and I did not have the strength to tell her that her baby brother would never come home. I tried to get off the subject so many times, but finally she loss interest and went away to play. Steve and I both tried to act to the girls like nothing was wrong, which was not easy! I had baby things lying all over the house, and everywhere I looked they were crying out to me.

I kept running my hand across my tummy; everything looked normal from the outside. I still looked very much pregnant. But I knew now that my son was dead inside of me. *How can I make it through this?* I kept asking myself over and over again. Sometimes I felt like I was going to fall apart. There just had to be a mistake; my baby had to be all right! I couldn't stop to think about everything that had just happened; there were too many things to do to keep me busy! As long as I kept myself busy, it didn't seem to be happening to me!

We got the girls ready for bed and tucked them in. We told them how much we loved them as always. But this night, I was having a hard time holding back the tears. A lump was forming in my throat as I was saying those words to my little girls. I knew in my heart I would never get to tuck my son into bed, or tell him how much I loved him. I kept trying not to think about it, but I could not stop myself! Something was getting ahold of my emotions, and I was so scared! I was always good at keeping it together so people wouldn't know what I was feeling, but I could not get control of this situation or my emotions; it was overtaking me!

Steve sat up with me for a while, but he just couldn't stay awake. I was having trouble falling a sleep, so I lay there thinking. Later, after Steve had fallen asleep, I got up and walked around the house. I even talked to God—something I hadn't done in a long time! Things just did not make any sense. How could God do this to me? I told Him that I would do anything for Him if He just wouldn't take my son away. I even got so brave as to tell God to take me instead of my son. I couldn't find it in my heart to believe that God could be so cruel. Why wasn't He hearing my prayers? "God," I said, "Please, please do something!"

Chapter 10

That was the longest night of my life! Steve had tried to be supportive, but he was hurting too. There was nothing I could do to make this all go away. I felt I had to tell Steve I was sorry all the time, and I blamed myself for what was happening. He kept telling me that I had nothing to feel sorry for, but inside I felt different. There was a big battle going on inside of me—one side knew I needed to be strong for my family, and the other side just wanted to fall apart. Which one was going to win was the question.

I sat up the whole night just thinking and talking to myself. I wanted answers but I didn't have any. I folded baby clothes and baby blankets. I looked at an empty bassinet...knowing that it would stay empty. I would look at my tummy from time to time in the mirror and touch it. I knew in my heart now that there was no little life inside of me. I kept crying; I could not seem to turn it off no matter how hard I tried! It all just hurt way too much! I can still feel that pain when I close my eyes and think about it. There are no words to explain that kind of pain, and there is no medicine to make the pain go away.

Before I knew it, morning came. Steve drove me to the hospital. They were already waiting for me in the labor & delivery room. Normally this is such a happy time, but it wouldn't be for me that day. No one seemed to be smiling, just long faces. I had several more tests done and was told by another doctor that my son had been dead inside of me for more than a week and was beginning to deteriorate. Could it get any worse, I thought to myself. But I didn't have time to worry about that because the doctors were getting concerned for my own health now.

My labor took twelve long hours—at least they seemed long to me. While I was in labor, I got a terrible pain down by my ovaries that had me scream out in terror. I had never felt anything like that before. It was as if a knife was being dug right into my stomach. All at once more doctors and nurses came flooding into the room. One was telling me he was giving me something for the pain as he shot something into my arm. Another was trying to talk to me calmly as he put an oxygen mask on me, telling me to take slow deep breaths. "What is happening to me?" I whispered to myself. But no one could hear my whispers above my cries of pain. I was being hooked up to more monitors, while my mind starting spinning out of control. I was only half there now; I could feel myself drifting away and nothing was making any sense to me. I knew the pain was overtaking me.

As my room was filling up with people, it seemed to me that everyone was moving at such a fast pace. My doctor had two nurses get stools and stand on both sides of me. From what I could hear them saying, the baby had gotten stuck inside the birth canal and was pushing on something. All at once both of the nurses dug their elbows into my stomach and began to push the baby out. I screamed out in pain! I was in so much pain, I thought I was going to die right that minute! After a period of time, they were able to get the baby out.

There was a stillness in the air when my little boy was born that I will always remember. There was no little cry to be heard, not a sound. Before he was born, while they were preparing me for labor, Steve and I were asked several questions. One of them was if we wanted to hold the baby. What?! Hold a dead baby? Were they kidding? What type of question is that to ask grieving parents? There was no way I could even think of doing that. Just the thought made me sick to my stomach! What was wrong with these people? Didn't they get it? How would I even be able to look at my dead baby? Didn't they realize how much I was hurting?

So we had our little boy. We named him Michael Steven. He was born at 5:51 p.m. and only weighed 2 pounds, 15.8 ounces. When he was born Steve looked right at me with tears running down his face and said, "I see Jesus holding Michael on His lap." I wondered where that had come from and why he said it. I had no idea just how important those words would become to me later in my life. They say that when a mother holds her baby for the first time after it is born, she forgets her pain from childbirth. I had no newborn baby to hold; I felt all my pain!

After Michael was born, I watched a nurse wrap him in a blanket just like she would a living newborn baby. She put one of those silly baby caps on him and laid him on the baby cart. Now, for some reason, I wanted to see my little boy. I asked the nurse if I could please see him. She looked so surprised, because I had been so much against it. She pushed the baby cart over by the head of my bed. The room had emptied out now except for this nurse. Steve told me he was having a hard time looking at Michael because it just hurt too much. I took a deep breath, knowing I had to do this. I knew in my heart that I needed to see my son, no matter how much it hurt!

Chapter 11

My little boy wasn't so pretty to look at, but he looked beautiful to me! His skin was beginning to deteriorate, because of how long he'd already been dead inside of me. I just kept looking at him. Then in my mind I began to speak to him. It was like I knew somehow he could hear me. *Michael,* I said, holding back the tears, *It's your mommy. I don't know how to say hello to you, and now I have to say good-bye.* I told him I loved him and how much we all would miss him. I said that he looked just like his sister Jennifer. I also told him not to be afraid, that he would be with Jesus now and that Jesus would take care of him for me—that one day we would all be together again. I told him how sorry I was that this terrible thing had happened to him. But most important, I told him how hard it was for me to say good-bye.

I tried to think of everything I wanted to say to him in just a few minutes. I had tears streaming down my face as I looked at him. Inside I felt like someone was tearing my heart right out of me! At the time, I think I was hoping he would open his eyes and look right at me, but he didn't. He just lay there on that cold cart and never moved. How could I say good-bye to him? How could I tell him how much he meant to me in just a short time? How would he ever know how much I loved him? When I thought of those questions, I found myself having trouble breathing.

Steve was having a really hard time with all of this. I felt so bad for him. Now was the time that I needed to be strong for him! I kept telling myself over and over again, *You need to get a grip, you can do this. You are strong...come on, pull your-self together...stop this crying!* I needed to remember how to push my feelings deep inside of me. I had always known how to survive, but I needed to remember how to do it again! I had learned the hard way when I was a teen not to let anything or anyone get to me. I could make it through anything, or so I thought. So that moment I decided I wouldn't let anyone see me fall apart. I would try my hardest to hold it all inside till I was alone! I had to make it through this—I was stronger than all of this! I would remind myself how to bury this pain deep inside of me.

After a period of time the nurse came back into the room. She told me she needed to take Michael—yes, she even called him by his name, which made everything seem even more real to me! I thought to myself, *Take him...but where to?* I couldn't even find the words to speak, so I just nodded my head. How do I describe what it was like watching my son being taken away from me forever? I blew him a tender kiss, and wiping a tear from my cheek I said, "Michael, I'll never forget you!" Then with tears streaming down my face out of control, I uttered the words outloud, "Don't forget me...I will always love you! I will see you again." I couldn't hold back the tears, no matter how hard I tried. The dam had broken! "Don't forget your mommy!" I said as she wheeled my little baby boy's cart out of the room. Then in the blink of an eye, my son was gone forever!

I just lay there listening to Steve crying. My tears had stopped as fast as they had started. My face was soaked from tears, I was drained, and I felt an emptiness I cannot put into words. It was like a part of me had been taken away. I was numb and cold inside and out! I wiped the tears from my eyes with my hospital gown. *How could God do this?* I thought to myself. *I will never forgive Him for taking my only son! Doesn't He hear my prayers? What did I ever do to deserve this?* I was becoming very angry and bitter with God. To me, at that moment, He wasn't a good God anymore. *My family doesn't deserve this,* I said to myself. *Why didn't He take me instead? Why my innocent little boy?*

So began my bitter feelings towards God. I didn't plan it that way, it just started growing inside of me and I couldn't stop it. I just couldn't understand why this had happened. I wanted answers, and because there were no answers I became very angry. I needed to blame someone, so God just happened to be the one I chose. Looking back, I cannot believe the many things I said to Him, but I believe God knew I was hurting and in pain from grieving and He gave me great mercy. I am so thankful that we have a merciful, forgiving God! He knows how we truly feel in a time of loss, and I believe in my heart that's the time when He is with us the most—even if we cannot feel Him because we are in so much pain!

My mom came into the room shortly after they had taken Michael out. She too was having a hard time dealing with all of this. She had just seen Michael and was now remembering my baby sister's death that had happened almost twenty-five years ago. I felt so sad for her! I could tell by her face that this had brought back all the memories of her own personal loss. My sister had only lived to be twenty days old. And I could remember what a hard time my mom had grieving for her. As I looked at her crying, I told myself, *I will never get over this pain; it will be with me forever. No one ever gets over anything like this. How can you deal with losing a child? How do you go on? What good can ever come from this?*

To me, it wasn't fair to see all the people I loved hurting so much. I tried to comfort everyone and tell them things would be all right. Who was I trying to fool? *Will my life ever be normal again?* I wondered. Somehow I knew deep inside that everything had changed in my life forever. *Where are you, God? Don't you care anymore about me?* I had no idea at the time that He was with me then more than ever!

Another nurse came back into my room and told me that they were moving me to a private room. I told Steve just to have everyone go home, and for him to go home and be with the girls. I said I just wanted some time to be alone. Actually, I wanted some time just to cry by myself and mourn my little boy. But there was no way I was going to tell anyone that!

Chapter 12

How could God take away my son? I couldn't understand, I couldn't help but be hurt. I asked Him how He could be so cruel, but I got no answer. I wanted to come face-to-face with Him. I had so many questions and I was demanding answers from someone. I just couldn't believe what was happening to me! I never heard any answers from God, so I figured He was afraid to face me. Didn't I realize who I was talking to? For some reason I just didn't seem to care. I couldn't get control of what I saying or the anger that was building up inside of me. It was like I was someone else.

I was told that all of the private rooms in the hospital were full, so I was put on the maternity floor with another patient. As I lay there in my bed, I could hear the newborn babies crying in the nursery. Their cries shot like an arrow, penetrating my heart. I fought to hold back the tears, knowing I would never hear my baby crying like that. The nursery was only a few doors down from my room, and I heard all their cries. I was sure I was being punished for something in my life and that someone was out to get me. Why was God punishing me in such a way as this? Nothing was making any sense to me. Why couldn't I wake up from this bad dream. I'd touch my stomach, which was still swollen, but empty. I knew I would have no baby to hold or cuddle. My breast milk had started to come in, but in vain. I felt so empty and so alone!

Finally...I cried myself to sleep. When I awoke, an elderly lady was standing by my bed. She introduced herself to me and said she was with a support group at the hospital. She told me a lot of things that day. I wasn't very good company; all I did was stare out the window as she talked. Nothing anyone could say could make this easier for me. She mentioned how the support group met and shared their feelings; that other parents had felt such a loss as this. She said when a baby is born dead they are called *stillborn*. It sounded so gross—people talking about their dead babies. What kind of help is that?

After a while she finally left my room. She must have noticed that I wasn't paying any attention to her. I was in my own little world. Before she had walked out, she left some booklets on my dinner cart and told me they might help me. Was she kidding? Help me? No one could help me. Didn't she see that? I just wanted to be left alone! After a while I began to look at one of the booklets called "When Hello Means Good-Bye." I got to the first page, then threw it on the floor. It talked about grieving for your child. *Gee, why don't they push the knife in a little deeper?* Didn't anyone understand how bad this hurt? Didn't anyone care? I couldn't deal with these kinds of people right now, my pain was too great.

Just then a nurse walked into my room and saw the booklet lying on the floor. She didn't say a word to me, but went right over and picked it up. She then gathered the other booklets that were lying on the dinner cart and laid them on a dresser that was near me. She quietly turned to me and with tears in her eyes said that it was all right for me to feel this way. That when I was ready, one day I would look at the booklets. That one day I would find my healing in all of this. I didn't say a word to her, I just went back to staring out the window. She then told me I needed to sign some papers for her.

The first one was Michael's birth certificate. As I looked at it, I felt a lump form in my throat. I knew I needed to find the strength to sign that form, and somehow I did. There could be nothing worse for me to do, or so I thought. She then removed Michael's birth certificate and replaced it with another form and

said, "You need to sign this form too. It is his death certificate."
I felt a cold chill go right through me. I held back the tears and
quickly signed it. I had no more strength left in my hand, and
the pen just fell to the floor. The nurse picked up the pen and
the last signed form and slowly walked out of the room. I just
sat their staring off into space. *It's over,* I thought. *It's all over.
Michael is gone, and a part of me is gone too!*

Chapter 13

After a while, another nurse came back into my room. She told me she needed to ask me several questions. *Don't these nurses get it? Why are they bothering me? I just want to be alone!* She told me it was the law to bury a child that was born dead. How could she think I wouldn't bury my child? Even if I hadn't taken the time to think about it, because I was hurting, I somehow knew I would have to face it! *Isn't a baby a human life?* I couldn't believe what I was hearing—these nurses were getting on my nerves! She explained that a funeral director would be coming to talk to me about arrangements for Michael. *When will all this end?* I thought to myself.

Steve and I talked about it and decided to have an autopsy done to find out the cause of Michael's death. We just couldn't understand what had happened. My doctor finally came in and checked on me. He said he was going to let me go home the following day. He then asked if I wanted any pills to help me cope with depression. Was he kidding? I wasn't depressed, I was angry! I could handle things just fine, I didn't need any pill. Why would he think I was getting depressed?

The next morning Steve came and took me home to my family. It felt so good to be out of the hospital. I looked out the car window as Steve was driving home. People were busy doing everything they normally did. The world had not stopped just because my son had died. I guess in my head I thought it would. I wanted to scream, but I didn't have the strength. Once I got home, my house felt cold and empty again. There were all kinds of people inside the house waiting for us. I wasn't even sure who they all were. When the girls saw me, they came running, and I went walking towards them to meet them. I loved my little girls, and I needed them now more than ever! Everyone I walked by kept telling me how sorry they were, but it just sounded like a broken record after a while.

I sat down and tried to play with the girls, but I felt empty inside. It was as if something or someone was missing in my life. I got up and tried to do some housework to get my mind off of things, but nothing seemed to help that feeling. Some of the people began to leave, but then others would come. Some people dropped off food, while others called on the phone. There were people everywhere I turned, yet I felt so alone! Some of them would just stare at me with tears running down their faces. They didn't know what to say to me, and the truth is I didn't know what to say to them either. How could I tell these people that I just wanted to be left alone? I would make sure the girls and Steve were fed every meal, but for some reason I had lost my appetite.

I did whatever I could to keep busy so I wouldn't have time to think about everything that had happened the last few days. I held it all together as long as I was busy and there were people around me, but the minute I was alone, I fell apart. I would hear babies crying when there were no babies around me. I kept feeling like I was losing my mind. I found it very hard to determine what was real in my life and what wasn't. I was losing touch with reality and I knew it. I just couldn't seem to get ahold of anything that seemed real to me.

One day I went downstairs to do a load of laundry and came across my son's newborn baby clothes. I grabbed a handful of them and just sat right down on that cold basement floor and held them. I knew I would have no baby boy to wear those clothes, and I closed my eyes and rocked back and forth, trying hard not to cry. They felt empty to me, the same as I was feeling inside. I just couldn't bring myself to put away any of the baby's things. It was really hard for me to look at the empty bassinet that sat in our bedroom, knowing in my heart that it would stay empty. I knew the baby things should be put away, but I was afraid to. My heart missed my baby boy so much! As long as his things were out for me to look at, I would never forget him! I thought that if I put everything away, it would be like he never existed.

I wanted my son, but there was nothing I could do to bring him back. I felt so helpless! My arms yearned to hold my baby boy. My whole body seemed to shake and cry out for him. It is a pain there are no words to describe. I'd look up to the sky and wonder where he was, and if he could see me. Somehow I just knew he could hear me. "Don't forget, I love you, Michael," I would say with tears swelling up in my eyes while I looked up at the fluffy clouds in the sky. "I'll never stop loving you!" I had no idea what to do or how to act. All I knew was this was the worst pain I had ever felt in my life, and it just wouldn't stop hurting!

Chapter 14

I was upstairs when I heard a knock at the door that went straight through me. I knew someone downstairs would get the door, so I just sat down on the edge of my bed and listened. I could hear an older man's voice as Steve greeted him at the door. Suddenly, Steve yelled upstairs for me to come down. I couldn't move my body to get up, so I yelled back and said I would be there in a minute. *I have to do this,* I told myself. I already knew in my heart who the man was; I just needed to find the strength to face him. I pulled myself together, wiped the tears from my face an slowly went downstairs.

When I walked into the living room, the man stood to his feet. He introduced himself to me as the director of some funeral home. He didn't catch me off guard, I had a feeling it was him. I took a deep breath as a lump formed in my throat! He was so sweet and really seemed to care about what we were going through. He handed us a book from which we could pick out a casket for our son, Michael. As I started looking through it, I could feel my whole body shaking out of control! The last thing you ever think of as a parent is that you will have to pick out your own child's casket. It was really hard for Steve and me to do, but we had no choice! We finally agreed upon a casket, then excused myself and said I would be right back. I told the funeral director I needed to get something for him upstairs.

In my bedroom was the baby's dresser. I opened a drawer and pulled out an outfit that I had planned on having my son wear home from the hospital when he was born. It was a white sleeper with pull strings at the bottom, and there were tiny little white lambs embroidered on the collar. I clutched the sleeper to my chest and fought back the tears with all my might. *Michael will look good in this,* I thought. I didn't want him to get cold, so I grabbed him a soft, woolly baby blanket that was laying in the bassinet. The blanket had little lambs on it and matched the white sleeper perfectly. As I was turning to walk out of the room, I spotted a stuffed woolly lamb on a shelf.

It was a gift a friend in Georgia had given me when Jennifer was born, and it played the song "It's a Small World After All." I grabbed the lamb and started the music. I no longer could hold back the tears—they just started flowing. I knew what I had to do; I just needed the strength to do it. These things needed to be buried with Michael, they were his now. I felt it was one last thing I could do for him, to show him how much I loved him! I could almost picture his tiny body in the sleeper!

I finally got control of myself and wiped the tears from my eyes. I walked slowly downstairs, clutching the items in my hands. I walked into the room where Steve and the funeral director were. I asked the funeral director if we could have Michael buried with these items. He looked so surprised at me and I saw tears begin to form in his eyes. He began to tell me how some parents didn't care how their stillborn babies are buried—that some are buried the same way they enter the world, with nothing on and no one caring anything about them. That some parents just want to act like it never happened. The thought of a little baby being buried that way made me start crying again. As he was leaving, I told the funeral director to take good care of my son, and he promised me he would.

Later that night when I should have been sleeping, memories of my baby sister's funeral began to flood my mind. I was about fourteen years old when she died. My mom had taken her death very hard—she always seemed to be crying. At the time, I really didn't understand why. There was a lot about her death and funeral that now came flooding back at me. She had only lived to be a few weeks old before she passed away and never came home from the hospital. I got to see her before she died, and I will never forget it. She had all kinds of tubes sticking out of her to feed her and help her breathe. I didn't understand what was wrong with her, I just knew she was very sick! She was so small, like a tiny little baby doll. I remember how tiny her casket was and how I felt the day we buried her. Then it hit me—*tomorrow I will bury my own son. He'll be the one in the casket.* It would be my final good-bye to him.

Chapter 15

I didn't sleep very well the night before the funeral. Every time I closed my eyes, I saw my son. The day of the funeral is still pretty much a blur to me. I was numb through the whole thing. I remember it was cold and rainy, and someone held an umbrella over my head as I walked from the car to the grave. I kept looking at the closed casket in disbelief. It was hard for me to believe that my son was in there. We had a pastor my mom knew do the service. He read some scriptures out of his Bible and a poem that I had given him to read. I wanted to have something special read at my son's funeral, so I found a poem in the booklet *When Hello Means Goodbye*. Yes, somehow I found the strength to look inside the booklet that had been given to me in the hospital.

Steve held Jessica, and I held Jennifer during the service. We had only a graveside service, as the funeral director had suggested. There would be no notice in the local newspaper of Michael's death till the next day so that there would not be a crowd at the grave. He told us that was usually the way things were done for stillborn babies. We were also told that when there is a stillborn baby buried, there is usually only a small family graveside service, but we had a lot more people there that day then probably was expected. I remember there only being seats for Steve and me. It was fine with me to have only a graveside service; I could not handle much more.

I began to hear someone crying behind me; I could hear them so plainly. I could tell they were having a really hard time coping with all of this. I could never stand to see anyone hurting, and now it seemed that everyone around me was hurting. I felt so badly for them. *When will all this pain stop? Haven't we all suffered enough?* I couldn't focus on anything that was being said by the pastor; it was just too hard and painful. So I began to look around at everyone. As I looked over at Steve, I saw he had tears running down his face. My heart sank just to see him that way. I knew our girls didn't understand what was happening. I was amazed at how good they were being through the whole service.

My mom was really having a hard time making it through the service. I am sure she was remembering her own loss, as well as now losing her grandson. I kept looking around at everyone who was there; they just looked so sad. I know my physical body was there, but mentally I wasn't. I remember I started talking to my son in my head as I looked back at the casket. I told him how much I would miss him and that I didn't know how to say good-bye to him. I began to feel the tears streaming down my face as I was talking to him. I was having my own private conversation with my son, telling him good-bye the only way I could. I asked him to watch over his sisters. I told him that I knew he wasn't really in that casket and that I could feel him watching us from up above. I kept saying his name over and over again in my mind. I just wanted to make sure he knew how much I loved him and would miss him.

The hardest thing of all was walking away from that casket, from his grave. As I was walking away, I slowly turned back and looked over my shoulder; it hurt me to know that now this would be the end...the real final good-bye! *Good-bye, Michael, I will love you forever and never forget you. I promise!* I couldn't get the lump out of my throat to utter the words out loud, but in my mind I was screaming them.

I finally turned my head around and kept walking blindly in the direction of the car. I could feel someone leading me, but I don't remember who it was. I was numb. I couldn't feel anything around me anymore, including the ground. I knew in my heart that it was time for his body to be put into the cold ground, and there was nothing I could do about it. When I thought about that, I felt myself getting sick to my stomach.

Neither Steve nor I could say a word to each other as we drove away. What really was left to say? Steve leaned over and grabbed my hand and squeezed it. It was his way of saying he was there for me. I knew he was hurting as much as I was as we were both telling our son good-bye. I quickly turned around to get one more look at the casket as we were driving away, but it was too late; it was nowhere to be seen. *It's over,* I thought. *It's all over! How do I go on from here?* My mind began spinning out of control, the same way it did the day the doctors told me Michael was dead inside of me. All at once I felt a warm tear run down my cheek.

At that moment everything started feeling very real to me. *Oh my God, I just had a baby, and he died! I don't have him anymore! He was taken away from me before I ever got to know him, before I ever got to hold him.* Reality was now hitting me like a ton of bricks in my face! *This isn't fair! This should never have happened! God, why did you do this? I want my son back! Do you hear me? I want my son back!* But no one could hear my screams inside my head. I was screaming only to myself! I had finally come to realize that this was really happening and that this cemetery was to be my little boy's new home.

Chapter 16

The funeral was over! The pregnancy was over! But the birth of my son was still very much present, and so was his death! Everywhere I went people kept telling me they were sorry and that in time I would feel better. Were they kidding? Feel better, how? They would tell me that time heals all wounds. I am sure they meant well by what they said, but they just did not understand what I was going through. Every minute, every hour was hard just to make it through. It was especially hard for me to see other moms holding their little babies. I knew in my heart I would never get to hold my little boy. Seeing those moms with their babies made it hurt even worse. I wasn't jealous of them, I just wanted my own little boy to hold. Was that so wrong? I would tell myself, *You can't run away from this. You have to learn how to deal with what has happened.* I then decided to keep myself as busy as I could so I wouldn't have time to think about or miss Michael.

I threw myself into my housework. Two days after the funeral I was doing laundry in the basement when I came across some newborn baby clothes in a brown paper bag. I had bought these clothes at a garage sale and had placed them down by the washer to be washed before the baby came. I began to pull each outfit out of the bag, then laid each one down in front of me in a pile. They looked lifeless to me—empty! As empty as I was feeling inside right now. I grabbed a handful of the tiny newborn outfits, plopped right down in the dirty laundry, and started crying. I needed to let it all out; I missed Michael so much! The pain was hurting more than I could bear, and I just couldn't hold back the tears anymore. The girls were upstairs playing and I knew no one would see or hear me crying. So right there, that day, in that dirty laundry, on that cold dirty basement floor...I let all my sorrow and all my tears flow out of me for my son.

I cried and cried and cried; I couldn't turn off the tears no matter how hard I tried. *Now maybe I will start feeling better*, I thought. I had stored up all the tears, and now they were releasing. I kept reassuring myself that I would be fine now. I am not sure how long I sat there and cried, but I cried till I couldn't cry anymore. Then I wiped the tears from my eyes with one of the outfits. When I realized what I was doing, I just smiled to myself and said, "At least this outfit got used!" I tried to make some humor of it all. When I went to stand to my feet, all at once I noticed that I had terrible pain in my left leg. I just thought maybe I had sat on my leg the wrong way and had a Charley horse or that my leg had fallen asleep.

But the pain wouldn't stop hurting, and it seemed to keep getting worse! I pulled up my blue jeans as high as I could to take a look at my left leg. I was shocked by what I saw! It was very swollen and totally discolored. I tried the best I could to stand to my feet, but my left leg just wouldn't hold me up when I put weight on it. I somehow limped my way to the stairs and crawled up the steps. By now I was starting to have more trouble breathing. I had terrible pain in my chest, and no matter how hard I tried, I just could not breathe right. It felt like something was pushing on my chest every time I took a deep breath.

Now I was getting really scared! I thought I was having a heart attack. I knew something had to be terribly wrong with me and that I needed help. Somehow I made it to the telephone in the kitchen and called Steve's work. But once again one of the secretaries told me Steve was working out of town. What was I going to do? I finally decided to call a friend of mine whose husband worked with Steve. I explained to her everything that was happening to me and told her I needed to get to the hospital right away. She told me to stay put, that she would be right over. I could see the girls playing in the next room, so I just sat on the kitchen floor watching them. They had no idea what was happening to me, and I wanted to keep it that way.

I called Steve's mom and asked if she could please come get the girls and take them to her house. I told her that Steve would pick them up later on after he got off work and then explained to her what was happening to me. I could tell by her voice that she was concerned. She said she would be there as fast as she could, that she needed to get a driver to bring her. Before I knew it, my friend came. The pain just kept getting worse, and there was nothing I could do to stop it.

Steve's mom arrived shortly after my friend, and they all helped me get into her car, because I could not walk on my own. Steve's mom told me not to worry. But how could I not worry—something was seriously wrong with me, I could feel it! I was sure I was dying! My friend rushed me to the hospital as fast as she could, and by the time we got there I was having even more trouble breathing. The pain in my leg was now unbearable. I could feel my heart beating in my leg, which made no sense to me.

Chapter 17

O nce we got to the hospital, my friend pulled up to the emergency room entrance, jumped out of the car, and went running inside for help. I guess she was as scared as I was! I just sat there helpless, unable to move. Every time I tried to move, I would scream out in pain. I leaned my head back on the headrest and closed my eyes. I tried to focus on my breathing, but I couldn't focus on anything because of the pain! The next thing I remember, two nurses were trying to help me out of the car and onto a gurney. The more they moved me, the more pain I felt. I couldn't stop crying because of the pain. Now my whole body was in agony!

They wheeled me quickly into a waiting emergency room. All at once the room started scrambling—doctors and nurses were everywhere. I could see what was happening as I kept looking around for someone to help me with the pain. I heard one doctor tell a nurse to give me a shot of something. I watched as everyone around me worked at a frantic pace. They began hooking me up to all sorts of monitors. In the distance I starting hearing my heart beating on one of the monitors. Another doctor came over and put an oxygen mask on me and told me to take slow, deep breaths.

I tried to get someone's attention to give me something for the pain, but for some reason I could not talk very loud. And no one could hear my whispers above the noise. A doctor leaned over me and asked where I was in pain, but I was unable to tell him. I can still see the doctor's face as he was looking at me, waiting for me to say something. But before I could utter a single word, his face began to fade away from me. I remember the pain in my chest and leg becoming unbearable! I was having trouble breathing now more than ever. Then all at once, the voices became muffled and the room became very dark.... I had blacked out.

When I awoke, I was still in a lot of pain. They had me on oxygen to help me breathe, and a nurse was standing beside me checking my blood pressure. I grabbed her hand to get her attention, then with all my strength and might I lifted my oxygen mask and said, "My leg, it hurts so much!" As I was telling her this, I lifted my left leg to show her which one. I couldn't lift it up very far because of the pain, but she got the point of what I was trying to say. She went running out of the room at once, then brought a doctor back in with her. He lifted the blanket off my legs and looked at me in disbelief. Now my left leg was bluish in color and had swelled twice as big as my right one. The doctor quickly walked over to the phone in my room and paged several people. All of a sudden my room was filled with doctors and nurses once again.

Next thing I knew, I was being wheeled down the hall for tests to be done. I told one of the nurses that I wanted my husband. She told me my friend was trying to locate him, and that he would be here very soon. I was so scared, and I felt all alone. I had test after test done, some of which were very painful and made me sick to my stomach from the dye they put in my bloodstream. After several long hours of tests, I was finally able to see Steve. He looked drained—he didn't need this! I couldn't help but cry as soon as I saw him. He kept asking me how I was. I'd lie to him and tell him I was fine. I knew I wasn't, but I didn't want him to worry.

Every time a nurse would come in to check on me, I would beg her for something for the pain, but no one would give me anything, and the pain was so intense. I tried to keep it together, but I could not stop crying. I just couldn't take much more! All we were told was that the doctor would be in soon, that they were waiting for the tests to come back. The clock in my room didn't seem to move—at least that's what it felt like that day for us. It was as if time just stood still! All we had was time, time to wait, time to worry, time to think about burying our son, and time to ask why.

Later on, a nurse came into the room and told Steve he needed to register me in the hospital. Steve and I just looked at each other, and without him saying a word to me, he left the room. I asked her what was wrong with me, and all she told me was that I wouldn't be going home. Didn't anyone understand me? I wanted answers, but no one would tell me what was wrong. After what seemed like forever, Steve came back into the room. We both just looked at each other in disbelief at what was happening. What could we say to each other?

Finally the doctor who had first seen me when I entered the emergency room came into my room. He told me that a specialist would be coming to see me very soon. *Why do I need a specialist?* I thought. Then the doctor began to tell us that my tests had showed that I had Deep Vein Thrombosis (DVT). I had no clue what that meant, so I told him to please explain. He said that I had developed blood clots deep in my veins and that these type of clots are very dangerous because they can break loose and travel through the bloodstream to the lungs and block blood flow in the lungs. Mostly all I heard was *blood clots*. I knew that no one lived through blood clots.

He told us that these clots were breaking down and traveling through my system, which is why I was having trouble breathing. Steve and I looked at each other. We both had heard stories of blood clots killing people. We couldn't believe what we were hearing! We had just buried our son, and now this! The specialist soon came after the doctor had left our room. He too described to us what a blood clot was and what was happening to me. He told me that I had a bad case of DVT. He also said that I had a pulmonary embolism, which is often life-threatening. He told me he was going to put me on a large dose of blood thinner called heparin and said that hopefully the heparin would start dissolving the clots right away. I wondered what he meant by "hopefully."

He then began to tell me that he had wanted to put me in Intensive Care, but that there were no empty beds. Looking at me softly, he said he had no choice but to put me on the maternity floor. Was he kidding? Had he forgotten I had just lost my baby? My mind began to spin out of control. *This can't be happening... it just can't!* He said that since I had just had a baby, they could take care of me better on the maternity floor. He also told me they were going to have to monitor me very closely so that I did not hemorrhage from the blood thinner. I was listening to what he was saying, but his voice seemed far away from me. My mind was still stuck on his words of me being put on the maternity floor. How in the world would I be able to handle that? I thought it couldn't get any worse for me. But I had no idea what was about to happen.

Chapter 18

O nce I was taken to my room, I sent Steve home to be with the girls. I told him I was tired, but really I just wanted to be left alone. I couldn't stop thinking about everything that had happened. Nothing in my life made sense to me anymore. I felt as if I was being punished by God. Every time I turned around, something went wrong. It had been that way in my life as a child, but I thought it was over now. I had finally found true happiness in my life and a reason to go on! Was it wrong for me to be happy? Was it wrong for something good to finally happen to me? All I wanted was to be happy with Steve, our children, and to have the perfect family. Family meant everything to me, because I never had it growing up. Was that so wrong to want? I had so many questions but nowhere to turn for answers.

A nurse came in and drew some blood out of my arm. She said that someone would be coming and doing this about every two hours to check my blood. I hated needles, so this was very hard for me to deal with. I was informed that the strong dose of heparin I was on was causing me to hemorrhage. *What else?* I thought. I could tell that the nurses were getting concerned about me. I was shutting down and had stopped talking to them. What else could I say to them? What else could anyone say to me? The hardest thing of all that night, though, was hearing the babies crying in the nursery that was down the hall from my room. I wasn't allowed to get out of bed for anything, so if my door was left open after someone walked out, I couldn't close it.

Chills would go through my body every time I heard a newborn baby cry!

Things couldn't get any worse for me, or so I thought. Later that same evening while I was lying there watching TV, a young nurse brought a newborn baby in to me. She thought it was my baby and had brought the baby for me to breast-feed. She was very cheerful, and as she drew closer to my hospital bed, I could hear her talking to me, but I don't know what she was saying. I think my body was going into shock from what I was seeing! All at once she stopped in her tracks. She must have noticed the look on my face. She then realized that she had made a terrible mistake.

I am not sure who felt worse at that moment, her or me, but when she realized what had happened she said over and over again, "I am so sorry, I am so sorry!" She was not nearly as sorry as I was! I felt a lump swelling up in my throat and tears swelling in my eyes. I felt my arms yearning more than ever before to hold my baby! She quickly ran out of the room with the baby in her arms as fast as she had entered. I looked at the doorway and said, "Sorry to disappoint you...but my baby is dead!" I could feel myself choking on the words as I was saying them. I am not sure if she heard me or not, but I did, and the words cut right into my heart like a knife! "My baby is dead," I said over and over again to myself. I couldn't feel anything but emptiness as I said those words out loud.

Then it happened—I began to feel depression setting in, but I really didn't care. I had no more fight in me, no more will to live. I was not very good company for anyone who visited me, and I spent a lot of time just staring at the walls. I stopped talking to people, even to Steve. What was there left to say? My doctor began to worry about me; I could hear him talking to the nurses about me being depressed and shutting down. After fifteen days in the hospital, he decided it would be best to send me home. He was afraid that I was slowly drifting away from everything that was real to me, and that I was giving up the will to live. Truth is, I was.

So I was sent home. I hadn't even been home for twenty-four hours when Steve had to rush me right back to the hospital. I had terrible pain down by my ovaries now. It seemed that my blood clots were moving at a very rapid speed, as I was later to find out from the doctor. I had developed several large blood clots from my femoral artery to my heart. Clots had developed in my right leg, and I even had two blood clots (the size of a pinhead) penetrate my lungs. The doctor couldn't believe what he saw when I was brought back into the emergency room. He kept saying, "This is very, very serious!"

I was taken out of the emergency room and of course rushed back up to the maternity floor. I just couldn't seem to get off that floor! But this time I was in the last room at the end of the hall; I wasn't anywhere near the nursery. I couldn't stand for anyone to touch my legs or my stomach without screaming out in pain. At times the pain was so bad, I thought I would pass out. They gave me what they could to help ease the pain, but nothing seemed to take it all away. I could no longer breathe on my own, so they had me on oxygen all the time. The doctor was unable to find a pulse in my left leg, and I could tell he was getting concerned. It was bluish in color again, and now so was my right leg. What had happened to me? Who was this person in so much pain? Sometimes I didn't even feel like me anymore.

Chapter 19

Several days passed before my doctor came to see me. He said he needed to talk to me about something very serious, then sat down on the edge of my hospital bed and began to tell me what I was facing with my health. I could tell it wasn't easy for him to start talking about it, but he had no choice. "Time is running out for you," he said boldly. "Something has to be done!" He told me I wasn't getting any better. How could I tell him that I already knew that? He then told me they no longer could find a pulse in my left leg.

It seemed that I had one of the worst cases of DVT he had ever seen. He said he was puzzled with me and wasn't sure what to do. He had talked to some other specialists about my case and was considering some suggestions they had given him for me. They could do surgery on me and put a screen in both of my legs above the knee. But he really wasn't sure if that would help me because of all the clots that were traveling so fast through my bloodstream. He also said there was a chance of me hemorrhaging on the operating table and dying during surgery. He paused, then said very softly, "I don't know if we can even save your legs anymore!"

He was considering amputating both of my legs—that I had so many blood clots in both of my legs that they were hoping to stop them from going any farther in my body. My left leg was now damaged; there was no longer a pulse in that leg. And it was starting to cause me more health problems, which was not helping things at all! My right leg was now following in the same pattern as my left leg. He said that my right leg pulse was getting weaker and weaker every day, just as my left leg had. If they amputated both of my legs up to the hip, I could of course hemorrhage through that operation as well.

He said he thought amputation might be the only way to go at this time. *What does he mean, he "thinks"?* I wondered. I never said a single word to him through the whole conversation; I just listened. After he was done talking to me, he told me he knew I had a lot to think about and a lot to talk to Steve about. "You really don't have a lot of time to think about this," he said as he was standing up to leave. "Something needs to be done soon, or you will die." He then laid a piece of paper that he had been holding down on my dinner cart and told me that I needed to look it over and sign it.

After he left I lay there, trying to take it all in. I was afraid to see what the paper said, so I just stared at it instead of picking it up. I think I was hoping it would disappear, but it didn't. I felt like I had been hit with a ton of bricks. Was this real? What had just happened? How could I decide a thing like this? I had always been very active, I loved keeping busy and being on the go all the time. How could I ever depend on someone else to take care of me? It just wasn't me. I just couldn't picture myself like that, not me.

I knew the pain in my legs wasn't get any better, but I had no guarantee that I would even make it through the surgery. Why would I want to take a chance like that? I never had any good luck, only bad luck. I knew I wouldn't make it through any surgery like that. My daughter Jennifer was just beginning to walk, and here I was missing out on it. I was missing out on everything, and there was nothing I could do about it! The last thing I had ever expected was for all this to happen to me. How could I just give up my legs like this? All I could do now was think, and my mind was racing so fast I couldn't keep up with it.

I knew I couldn't take any more pain and that I couldn't take seeing my family suffer through all of this. I was missing my little girls so much! I missed being a wife; I missed having a normal life. What had happened? How did all my dreams get shattered? Things weren't suppose to end up this way. This was not what I saw my life becoming. I used to be full of energy, full of life. Now here I was, lying in this hospital bed, in this cold dark room, unable to get up, unable to walk. Not knowing if I would ever walk again. Not knowing if I would live or die by tomorrow. In the blink of an eye, my whole life had changed in more ways than one.

I picked up the paper the doctor had left on the dinner cart. All I remember is seeing the word *amputation*. I let the paper drop to the floor. *I can't do this! This is all just too much for me—I'm better off dead!* I no sooner uttered those words than my mind started thinking about my son, Michael. I missed him so much! He was dead, gone from me forever! I thought about Steve, the girls, and what I was putting them all through. *Enough is enough! I can't take any more!* That minute I made up my mind—I was going to wait everything out. I wouldn't have any surgery done. I also knew I couldn't take much more pain either. I knew something would finally have to give.

After a while, the doctor came back expecting to find a signed paper, but I wasn't about to sign it! He looked at me shocked and said, "Don't you understand that if you don't have this surgery, you will die?"

I had been having so much trouble breathing due to the blood clots that had penetrated my lungs. Even talking sometimes was very hard for me to do! I took a deep breath, found the strength to talk, and looked the doctor right in his eyes and said, "I don't want you to tell my husband any of this. I want to tell him myself."

The doctor just looked at me and shook his head. "You need to rethink this," he said. "I will check back with you tomorrow. Maybe you will change your mind." As he was heading out of my room, I answered him harshly, "I won't!"

Everyone has a breaking point, only so much a person can take, and I had reached mine! I had just buried my son, and now here I was being told that they wanted to amputate both of my legs. And better yet, that I could die if they didn't. I had been through more than my share, and I had tried to make it through. How much could one person take? I had had enough! I just didn't have any more strength in me to go on. The doctor had no idea what I was going through mentally. I had made up my mind, and I was sticking to it! Now I needed to focus on figuring out how I would tell Steve everything. How would I tell him good-bye? How could I tell him that I was done fighting to stay alive?

Chapter 20

That same afternoon Steve came to see me. I could tell he was tired, I could see it in his eyes. Here he was working a job, trying to take care of our house, taking caring of our two little girls, and trying to deal with a wife who was in the hospital in pretty bad shape. It was taking its toll on him! When he saw me, he smiled and came right over to me and asked how I was doing. What could I tell him? Steve always gives me a kiss when he leaves me, and he always gives me a kiss when he sees me. As he bent down to kiss me, I felt a tear run down my cheek. I knew I had to tell him everything the doctor had told me. I couldn't put it off anymore.

As he sat down on the bed beside me, I began to tell him everything. He just held his head down and looked at the bed so that I couldn't see his eyes filling up with tears. He didn't realize that I knew him very well, that I knew it would be hard for him to hear all of this. I told him about the piece of paper the doctor had given me to sign for the amputation and that I had refused to sign it. I could tell he was not impressed by what I was telling him.

He suddenly looked up at me, his eyes soaked with tears, and said very sternly, "You have no choice but to sign it." I know he meant well by what he was trying to tell me to do. But he knew me too and could tell by the look on my face that I had already made up my mind not to sign that paper! I had always been very headstrong, and he knew it. Once I put my mind to something, that was it, no one could change it.

Then I told him what the doctor had said about me dying if I did not have the surgery. Steve said I had no choice but to have the surgery so I could live. That is where I knew he was wrong; I did have a choice. I explained to him there was no guarantee that I would even make it through the operation. I told him I was not going to have the surgery, that I couldn't see me going through my life with my legs amputated. It just wasn't going to happen! I said that we would wait and see what would happen to me. Truth is, I guess we both knew in our hearts which way all of this was heading, we just didn't want to admit it to each other.

I knew that I needed him now more than ever. Steve could help me make it through anything, but I wasn't sure if we could make it through this one or not. It seemed like all of our luck had just run out. The room suddenly got very quite. I guess we were both thinking about what I had just said. I then quietly spoke up and told him that I needed to ask him something. He just sat there very quiet beside me on the bed, holding my hand and looking down at it. Very slowly I began to speak. "Steve, I want you to promise me something." Then, fighting back my tears, I said, "I want you to promise me that you will remarry if anything happens to me." He looked up at me suddenly, like someone had slapped him. Before he could say anything I blurted out quickly, "I don't want you to be alone if anything should happen to me. I need the girls to have a mommy."

He had tears running down his face now as he was looking at me and told me to stop talking like that. But I had to let him know—I had to tell him what I wanted him to do while I still could. It was my way of saying good-bye to him. I loved him so much, and the thought of him being alone was just too much for me to bear. I needed him to promise me that he would do this. I knew that if he promised me, he would never go back on that promise. I said, "I want you to give the girls a good home filled with lots and lots of love!" He just shook his head at me as he looked back down at my hands he was holding. I knew he didn't want to hear what I was saying, but it had to be said. He told me I was stuck with him, that I could not get rid of him that easy!

But I ignored what he was saying and kept right on talking. "I don't want her to look anything like me. She needs to be heavy, and have dark hair," I said jokingly, trying to hold back the tears. But Steve didn't get think it was funny; he wasn't laughing. He knew I had always been a fighter, and he couldn't understand why I had given up so easily. He didn't realize that I had no more strength in me to fight. I was drained, mentally and physically. I didn't have the strength to tell him that I just wanted everything over, including my life.

Steve and I sat there in silence for the longest time. There was nothing else left for me to say. It was all I could do not to fall apart crying in front of him, but I had to hold it together till he was gone. In my own way I had told him I loved him, and I had told him good-bye. He held my hands as my heart was breaking in two.

Looking back now, I believe that Steve and I felt more love for each other in that dark hospital room that day than we ever had before! Every once in a while I would see him wipe the tears from his face. It tugged at my heart to see him crying. I think he didn't know what to say to me, and I really had nothing more to say to him.

How do you let someone know how much you love them, and then tell them good-bye? When he would look at me I could see the pain in his eyes, but what could I say to make it all go away? I remember wishing that I would just go to sleep and never wake up. Finally I told Steve that he needed to go home and be with the girls. I knew they didn't understand any of this and they needed one of us to be there for them. I asked him if he would bring the girls to see me the following day. Boy, did I need to prepare myself for that one! But I wanted to tell my babies good-bye in my own way. I knew that I was dying, and I didn't know how much time I had left.

Steve sat with me a little longer, then decided to go home. I think he just wanted to spend some time alone to think about everything I had said to him. It was a lot to take in! After he left I just lay there and cried for the longest time. I began to battle with my all of my emotions, but the one that was the strongest was the anger I had with God for what He had done to me and my family. To me, God had forsaken me...and now I would forsake Him! Maybe He wasn't even real after all. Maybe the memories and stories I had heard about Him as a child had all just been lies. I looked up at the ceiling with tears streaming down my face and said loudly, "God...where are you? Why are you doing this to me?"

Chapter 21

As I was lying in bed telling God what I thought of Him, my phone rang. It was the woman who had brought me into the hospital—the one whose husband worked with Steve. She told me that both her and her husband were strong believers in God. *Great!* I thought. *What is she going to do, talk to me about God?* Now would not be the time to do that. She said Steve had told her husband what I was going through and that she had put my name on the prayer chain of their church. She also said that my name was on the prayer chain of a lot of churches in the area—that I had a lot of people praying for me. I should have been deeply touched, but I wasn't. All her words just seemed empty to me!

Then she mentioned that her pastor wanted to know if he and the elders from their church could come see me. Was she kidding me? What could they possibly do for me? I started to say no, that I didn't want them...but somehow a "yes" came out of my mouth before I knew what I was saying. *Great, just what I need is a bunch of crazy church people preaching to me about God. Boy, will I tell them a thing or two!* She then told me she would put a call in to her pastor right away and that they would all be coming to see me that night. *What? Why tonight?* "Oh well, let them come. I have nothing more to lose. Those elders better not preach to me about God, or I will get in their face!" I said out loud to myself. I thought I was too fargone for anyone to help me, let alone for God to care.

I just lay there waiting, thinking, taking in everything that had happened to me the last few weeks. When a knock came at my hospital room door, it brought me back to reality. I looked in the direction of the door and said as loudly as I could, "Come in." I couldn't believe what I was seeing, as in walked a large group of people. I think there was about twelve in all. My friend stepped toward me and placed some daffodils that were in a small Mason jar on my dinner cart. She then introduced each person to me, along with the pastor. I was so overwhelmed by that many people, I couldn't even remember their names. She said that these people were the elders of her church and that they had all been praying for me. I didn't have the heart to tell her that I didn't even know what an elder was.

She then mentioned to me that one of the elders felt the Lord telling him that they should come pray over me right away, and that they should not wait another day. I chuckled to myself and thought, *You're kinda late, don't you think? God stopped hearing my prayers weeks ago, maybe even years ago. It's over. God doesn't care anything about me.* Just then someone stepped forward and gave me an Amplified Bible and said it was a gift for me to keep. Someone else in the group spoke up and asked if I was saved. *What kind of question is that to ask someone?* I thought. Couldn't they tell that I was? I answer very sharply, "Of course I am saved! I was saved as a young girl, and once saved always saved." I couldn't believe how I was speaking to them...and to a pastor. What was I thinking? I didn't want to be mean, I was just fed up—fed up with everything! And I wasn't in the mood for anyone to talk to me about God. They never condemned me for my attitude or corrected me for how I talked to them. They just stood there looking at me, smiling. I tried to be nice and smile back at them, but it was too hard for me; I had nothing to smile about. Someone asked me if I believed the Lord could heal me. Without even thinking, I answered back, "If He wanted to, He could." Somewhere deep inside of me, I knew the Lord could heal. I had a memory locked deep inside and pushed back by pain and hurt.

He had touched me once, when I was a young girl. I had been healed at a tent meeting from a terrible bike accident. A man had prayed over me at that meeting, and I was healed. I had felt a warm feeling go through my entire body that night. I knew that I had felt the Lord! Even though I was young, I never forgot that experience the whole time growing up; I just buried it deep inside of me. Even through all the years that went by, I still remembered.

Yes, there had been a time when I was young that I had asked Jesus into my heart. I loved Jesus so much back then and I had wanted to be just like those preachers at the tent meetings my mom had taken me to. But now I had drifted far, far away from the Lord. Things stopped making sense to me when God didn't answer my prayers when I was growing up. I had a hard life growing up and had cried out to God for help, but He never answered those prayers. I had to grow up really fast, and I saw the world for what it is. Nothing I had been taught about God made sense to me. God changed to me, so I just stopped praying and reading my bible.

Yet I knew in my cold heart that night that GOD COULD HEAL! Not because someone told me He could, but because I had once experienced It. I just didn't want to talk about it—why should I? God didn't usually answer my prayers back then, nor did He now. I didn't want anyone to talk to me about God, about Him caring. I was mad at God! He didn't care; He hadn't answered my prayers! He didn't give my son back, He took him away from me! I quietly said to myself, "He doesn't love me or care anything about me." The pastor suddenly looked at me and asked if they could pray with me. "Sure, why not," I said. "I have nothing more to lose!" I knew that sooner or later they would ask to pray with me, which is what these types of people do, and I figured the sooner they prayed over me, the quicker they would leave.

One of the gentlemen from the group stepped forward and opened my Amplified Bible. He said, "I want to read you a scripture that I feel very strongly is for you." He read James 5:13–15: "Is anyone among you afflicted (ill-treated, suffering evil)? He should pray. Is anyone glad at heart? He should sing praise [to God]. Is anyone among you sick? He should call in the church elders (the spiritual guides). And they should pray over him, anointing him with oil in the Lord's name. And the prayer [that is] of faith will save him who is sick, and the Lord will restore him; and if he has committed sins, he will be forgiven." At the time, I thought they were just empty words from a book that someone was reading. I had no idea that those words would become very real to me!

Chapter 22

One of the elders told me they were going to anoint me with oil. I had seen this happen before at the tent meetings, but I did not know what it all meant. Weird thing, though, I wasn't scared about it! Maybe I was too far gone mentally to care anymore. Truth is, I really don't remember. One of the men from the group pulled out of his pocket a small clear bottle filled halfway with liquid and opened it. He then passed it around to each person, and each one of them put a little oil from the bottle on their fingertips. Yes, I was watching everything they were doing. Some of the people started praying right away, even before they had their bit of oil.

When the oil came to the pastor, he came right over to me and applied some oil on my forehead in the symbol of the cross and spoke some words over me. After he did this, some of the elders moved toward my bed and started praying. Needless to say, all of this was feeling a little weird to me. Some of them laid their hands on me, while others just prayed right where they stood. I watched closely as they closed their eyes and began to pray even louder. I didn't want to feel like an outcast, so I closed my eyes too. But I didn't pray, I just listened to every word they were saying. All at once I heard a couple of the people start speaking in tongues. I had heard that language people call "tongues" in the tent meetings and at some churches my mom had taken me to when I was a young girl.

I had asked my mom what the people were saying, and she told me that it was a prayer language between them and God.

Even though I never knew what they were saying, I always thought it was beautiful. But I had never heard anyone speaking in tongues that close to me before. I remember feeling very uncomfortable about the whole thing. *What are they doing?* I wondered. *Why are they praying so strongly?* Some of them kept getting louder, speaking like they were telling someone or something off. *Why are they acting like they are in a fight or a battle? Who are they talking to like that?*

I had no sooner started thinking about those things, when suddenly something very weird started happening to me! The top part of my body became very hot, and the bottom part of my body became very cold. *That's weird,* I thought. Then my legs began to thump and hurt worse than ever before. I could feel my heart racing at a fast pace as my whole body started shaking. *What is happening to me?* I wondered nervously. I wanted to tell them to stop praying—that they were making things worse for me—but for some reason, I could not open my mouth to speak. I wanted to push the button to page a nurse, but my hand wouldn't move. I just lay there helpless, and I was starting to panic.

I tried to figure out what was going on, but nothing made any sense to me. Every time they would raise their voices in prayer, the pain would get worse! How weird was that? I kept hearing words over and over again in my head, screaming out at me, "You're going to die, you're going to die! Tell them right now to stop praying!" What happened next caught me totally off guard. All of a sudden, my bed started shaking uncontrollably. It was shaking so hard that I was afraid I would fall to the floor! *Why are they trying to scare me? Why are they shaking my bed like this? This isn't how you are suppose to pray over people! You are not suppose to scare them when you pray! You can stop praying for me anytime now.* I had my eyes so tightly shut that I had tears running down my face.

Finally I was able to move my hands and grab hold of the mattress. I squeezed both sides of the mattress so tight that I could feel the edges curl up under my fingertips. I had to grab hold of something to keep from falling off the bed. I was so sure at any moment I would just fall. When I thought things couldn't get any more weird...they did. I know my eyes were tightly shut, but somehow I saw a corner of my hospital room. Don't ask me how, because I don't know...I just know I did! In the corner was a dark mist the color of charcoal, like a dark smoke. I could see it very plainly.

I tired to figure out what it was and how it had gotten there. When all at once that dark smoke turned into a shadow, a silhouette of a person. As soon as I saw it happen, I felt a cold chill go right to my bones. I had never felt anything like that before! This wasn't in a movie, it was actually happening! Next thing I knew, it felt as if that black mist was right on top of me. There was a pressure over my entire body, as if someone were lying right on top of me in a dead weight! *This is impossible,* I thought. *Nothing is here, this isn't real!* I was no longer just scared, I was now terrified! My mind was racing a mile a minute, trying to figure out what was happening. But there were things going on at that very moment that I could not explain.

I could feel my heart racing; it felt like it was going to burst. The pain was unbelievable! I thought to myself, *This thing on top of me is trying to kill me! How can this be happening? This can't be real....* Yet it was happening, and there was nothing I could do to stop it. I felt as if this thing on top of me was sucking my very life right out of me. In the distance I could hear the people in the room singing and praying. I didn't understand why they sounded like they were drifting away from me. I had terrible pressure in my head now; I knew something was terribly wrong. I started screaming inside my head for someone to help me, but no one could hear me. My screams were in vain as I lay there in my own torment!

I had no idea what was happening to me or how I was seeing what I was seeing. All of a sudden, I felt a terrible pain go straight to my heart like I had never felt before. My body jerked as I tried to take a deep breath. I felt strongly that if I didn't do something soon, I was going to die right that minute. All at once I heard myself cry out, "God...God, please help me, I don't want to die! Please...forgive me!" I felt a lump form in my throat, and my eyes fill with tears as I said His name in my head. Even though I was so mad at Him, I knew in my heart to call on His name! Something very weird was happening to me, and somehow I knew He was the only one who could help me.

Chapter 23

I felt myself gasp for more air, then suddenly the pain stopped. I couldn't see because my eyes were shut, yet somehow I saw the foot of my bed. First I saw a bright light appear, as if someone had turned this overwhelming bright light on in my room. Then I saw two of the most beautiful angels appear out of nowhere and walk straight to the foot of my bed. They just looked at me and smiled and reached out their hands and touched my toes. All at once, a sensational heat went through my entire body! It was as if someone had wrapped my body up in a heating pad and turned it on hot. I felt my body inside becoming so hot, yet it wasn't a burning feeling. It was a powerful warmth, like I had never felt before! It was rushing through my entire body, starting at my toes.

As soon as they touched me I felt the pressure that had been on top of me leave. I could feel the warmth going all the way through me, and the coldness that had been in the room disappeared. The room started feeling very warm, yet it was very comfortable! Then with my eyes still shut, I saw my entire room fill up with the bright light, and I could feel heat from the room on my eyelids. I remember trying to figure out what was happening, what I was truly feeling and seeing. *Could angels really be here in my room?* I wondered how that could be. My mind was filling up with so many questions, yet I could feel an overwhelming peace coming upon me.

I just had to know what was happening, so I quickly opened my eyes. But when I did, I saw nothing at the foot of my bed. *Where did they go?*

I looked all around the room, but the angels were nowhere to be seen. All I saw in my room were the elders and the pastor with their eyes closed, still praying. I closed my eyes quickly to try to see if I could see the two angels again, but nothing. They were gone. What had I seen? Was it real or was it my imagination? I opened my eyes and tried to focus so I could see the room more clearly. I felt like I was in a daze, like I had just woken up from a sound sleep. I could still feel the heat going through my body; it hadn't stopped. Even though I didn't see the angels anymore, to me it still felt like they were there.

For some reason the elders were standing across the room from my bed. To this day I still have no idea why they stood so far away from me. I must have had a funny look on my face, because one of the elders asked if I was all right. I looked myself over and replied, "I don't know." Truth is, I really didn't know. I looked over at the faces of the elders and the pastor, and they were all glowing. There was this feeling in my room that I had not felt before. All my worries were gone. Then it hit me—I realized that I had no pain anywhere in my body. For the first time in many, many weeks I had no pain!

I began to tell them that I had no more pain, but they didn't seem at all surprised by what I was saying. *They just don't understand,* I told myself. *How can this be? How can all my pain be gone—just like that?* They kept smiling back at me, and one person said loudly, "Praise the Lord, you are healed!" As soon as he uttered those words, the others started shouting and cheering. They were all so excited for me! I tried to get a hold on what was going on, but I couldn't. I didn't understand what had just happened to me, but they obviously did! *Why are they so happy for me? They don't even know me. Why do they care about me like this? What is it with these people?*

I began to explain to them what I had felt when they were praying for me—how I had felt hot, then cold. I asked them why they had shaken my bed. A couple of them looked at me, puzzled, and someone said, "No one shook your bed." Then I remembered that when I had opened my eyes, they had been standing across the room. One of the men said to me, "There is no way we could have shaken your bed, it's on wheels." I leaned over my bed and looked underneath it—sure enough, my bed had wheels. *Huh, that's weird!* I knew someone or some*thing* had shaken my bed. I had almost fallen off, it felt so real!

I then looked at the edges of my mattress where I had grabbed hold, and they were curled up just a little bit. It did happen, *I am not going nuts! It was real!* I began to notice that I had tears streaming down my face, and I hadn't even realized it. *What is happening to me?* But before I had time to even think about that, one of the elders said it was time for them to go. We all joined hands and gave a prayer of thanks to God. This time I closed my eyes, not because I had to, but because I wanted to. As someone prayed, I said my own personal thanks to God for what had just happened. All of a sudden I realized I didn't want them to go. I didn't want this feeling I had to leave with them.

Every one of them leaned down and hugged me and told me a gentle good-bye. As one gentleman was walking out the door, he turned around and said, "Your son is a little angel up in heaven now. Today the Lord touched you in a way you will never forget! A battle for your life happened here today. You don't understand all of this right now, but one day you will. When it is time, you will be able to help many people with your testimony! One day all of this that you have been through will be turned around to glorify the Lord! You have been healed today; your sins have all been forgiven." Before I could say a word to him, he turned and walked out of my room.

I just lay there staring at the doorway. What did he say? He had seen my son? Tears were streaming down my face. How... how had he seen my son? What did he mean, one day I would understand? Why did he say my son was a little angel? To me, my son already was a little angel. I hadn't told anyone what I felt in my heart, not even Steve.

I had no idea at the time why the man had said those words to me before he walked out of my room, and I never saw him again. I don't even know his name or the names of the people who came to see me that night, but I will never forget them, nor what that man said to me that day.

Chapter 24

For a while after everyone left, I just lay there trying to take it all in. I couldn't believe what had happened. It seemed like a dream, yet I knew it wasn't. It really had happened! I waited for my legs to start hurting, but they never did. I waited to start having trouble breathing, but I was breathing just fine. I knew something had happened to me, because I felt different inside. I tried to lay there and make sense of it all—the shadow I saw in the corner, the bed shaking, the two angels I had seen, and the heat that was still going through my body. There just had to be an explanation for what had happened! But what was it?

Then I realized I had bent over the bed to look under it to see if it had wheels. I hadn't been able to move like that in weeks. I bent over again. "Oh my gosh, I can move! I can move...I have no pain!" I said loudly, chuckling to myself. "I can move! What in the world is happening to me? I gotta call Steve and tell him what is happening." So I called Steve at home and told him everything that had happened. I probably talked a mile a minute, but I didn't care. There was so much to say! How could I explain to him what had happened to me and what I was feeling? I did the best I could to tell him, but I could tell by his voice he didn't believe me. He just listened and kept saying over and over again, "That's nice. He had no clue what had just happened to me.

I found out weeks later that he had thought they had given me too much pain medicine and that I was tripping out that night. I must have really sounded way out there to him, but I couldn't get over how happy I was! I felt something I had never felt before—I felt so alive! After I got off the phone with Steve, a nurse came in to give me my pain shot. I was scheduled to have one every couple hours; without it the pain had been almost unbearable. As she walked closer to my bed, I looked at her and said, "I don't think I need that shot, I have no more pain." She looked at me, surprised. "What do you mean?" she asked nervously.

I then began to tell her how the Lord had healed me...that I didn't need the shot. She didn't say a word to me, but just turned and walked right out of my room. After she left, I thought about what I had said to her. I had told her "The Lord healed me." I don't know if I really knew what I was saying or not. All I knew for sure was that I had no more pain—not even a little bit. It was all gone! *I am healed!* I realized. *I am healed....oh my gosh, I think...I am healed!* Could God actually have healed me? Wow, talk about taking something in. What can a person say to that? How are you suppose to act?

I started to unhook myself from the monitors I was hooked up to. I removed the oxygen tube from under my nose that had helped me breathe. "Yep, I can breathe just fine!" I said as I giggled to myself. I couldn't help but start laughing. I had this overwhelming feeling of joy deep inside of me! "I never did like needles, I don't need this anymore," I said out loud as I was trying to pull out the IV needle. Alarms and buzzers started going off everywhere in my room. Suddenly my room filled up with nurses. They asked what I was doing. I looked at them and boldly said, "I am healed; I don't need to be hooked up to this stuff anymore!"

They all just looked at each other and walked over toward my bed and told me to just calm down. How do you calm down after something like that happens to you? I'm sure they thought I was going nuts. If they had only known what really happened to me! I even remember one of the nurses saying, "Sweetie, you are dying, and you need to stay hooked up to all of these monitors."

"No I don't," I answered back, laughing at her. "I have no more pain and I can breathe just fine!" The nurses were frantically trying to get me to stop unhooking myself, but it wasn't working. I wanted up out of bed!

Finally one of the nurses noticed that I was breathing just fine on my own without the oxygen tube under my nose. Everyone stopped in their tracks when she said, "Look—she *is* breathing normally! She can breathe on her own."

"I told you so," I said, smiling back at them. "I will stop unhooking everything if you will call my doctor and tell him I want to see him right away. I want out of this bed!"

One of the nurses said she would go and call the doctor for me, and she walked out of the room. Another nurse pushed the IV needle that was starting to fall out back into my arm. "Just lie still," she said. "The doctor is being called."

I stopped moving around and just lay there, letting the nurses hook me back up to the monitors. "You'll see," I said quietly. "I am healed."

Soon the nurses left my room after making sure everything was hooked up just right. I was still feeling the heat going through my entire body. But now I was feeling something even stronger—an overwhelming peace falling upon me. I closed my eyes to relax, and I must have fallen a sleep. When I woke up, I tried to tell myself it had all just been a dream. I rolled over on my side, not even thinking about what I was doing, when it hit me—I had not been able to roll over on my side for the longest time. I smiled to myself and said, "It really did happen—God really did heal me!" I then looked toward my dinner cart and noticed the Bible that had been given to me just lying there. I leaned over and picked it up.

The room was very still as I looked at the outside of that Bible for a long time. I was afraid to open it. Then slowly I started to get the courage to look inside. I hadn't read a Bible in a very long time. As soon as I thought about that, I felt an overwhelming sadness. I closed my eyes and asked God why—why did He heal me after all the terrible things I said to Him? I began to cry; I couldn't help myself. I felt so guilty for everything I had said and done, and I had no excuses for my actions! In that moment, while I was holding my Bible, I asked God to forgive me. With tears streaming down my face, I softly said, "Thank you, Lord, for not giving up on me!"

Chapter 25

Before I knew it, my doctor came to see me. He walked right into my room and sat down on my bed. "What's going on?" he asked, looking very concerned. "What is this I hear, that you want up?"

How do I begin to tell him what happened? Suddenly I blurted out, "God healed me, and I want out of this bed!"

He looked at me, astonished. "Tell me what happened," he said, curious.

I told him that a group of elders from a church had come to see me a few hours before and that they had prayed over me to be healed. I felt a tear run down my cheek as I said softly, "I know how weird this all sounds, but I actually got healed. I have no more pain anywhere in my body!"

He didn't say a word to me, he just got up and walked over to check my monitors. He unhooked my oxygen to see if I could breathe on my own, and I could. He checked my vital signs; they were all normal. He checked for a pulse in both of my legs; I now had a normal pulse. He then compressed on my femoral artery as he had done before, but this time I didn't scream out in pain! Every once in a while he would glance at me, still not saying a word. He compressed my legs to see if I would yell, but I didn't. I had no pain anywhere!

He then looked at me, puzzled, and said, "Sometimes unexplainable things happen to people." Was he kidding me? I knew this was explainable...the Lord had healed me!

I could tell that the doctor could not believe what he was seeing right in front of his eyes. He said he wanted to do some tests, but as for now he didn't see any reason I couldn't get up and walk around. He told me that they would take me off all the monitors, but that the IV had to stay in. *Fine by me. I will push my IV pole anywhere I want to go.* I had been in bed for over a month, so he said that I needed to take it very slow getting up.

When I first got up and put my feet over the side of the bed, they felt funny. When I went to stand up, I got very dizzy and had to sit right back down. But that didn't stop me. Finally I was able to stand to my feet and move around little by little.

A nurse unhooked my IV so I could take a shower. I can't explain how *fantastic* that shower felt—it was probably the best shower I ever had in my life! After getting cleaned up, I felt amazing. I wanted to leave my room and go walking. All I had seen was my room for weeks and I was ready to venture out. I paged the nurse and asked her to come hook my IV back up and if I could go walking down the hall. She said I could as long as I felt up to it. Was she kidding? Did I feel up to it? I had so much energy, I was ready to be let loose! There was no way anyone was going to keep me down. I was ready to run a marathon, or so I thought.

I stood in the doorway of my room and looked down the long hallway. Then I said out loud to myself, "You can do this..." I took a deep breath, pushed my IV pole forward, and took a tiny step into the hall. I felt weird, a little unbalanced from being down for so long. I took another deep breath, and reassuring myself I said, "You are healed. Now walk, and believe!" So I pushed my IV pole forward and put one foot in front of the other and began my walk. My feet were moving very slowly, like an old slow-motion picture. That was weird for me, because inside I was running non-stop! But my body was having a hard time keeping up with my spirit. I really didn't care—at least I was up and walking.

When I would pass the nurses' station, they would all just look at me. They were so surprised by the way I was now acting. And who could blame them—let's just say, I had not been the nicest person to them. But now something had happened to me, and I was so happy! It was like I was a completely different person. I would wave and say hello every time I would pass by a nurse. Looking back, they had to have thought I had finally lost my mind. But I had this joy all over me and I could not contain it. I had more determination in my heart than ever; I was going to beat this DVT. I was going to be better than I ever was before!

As I was walking, I would think about everything that had happened to me. I had been touched by God Almighty; I had actually felt Him! As impossible as it all sounded, it had happened! I started remembering all the prayer meetings and tent meetings my mom had taken me to when I was young. I had seen people healed there; I knew these things were possible, but somehow I had forgotten everything.

The Lord had been real to me once, but I had drifted far, far away from Him. I had once believed in the Father, the Son, and Holy Spirit. How had I forgotten? It was at that very moment that I realized I needed to give my life back to the Lord. I closed my eyes and quietly said, "Lord, please come walk with me." I felt tears fill my eyes as I said those words out loud to myself, words that came from my heart. I knew I needed the Lord in my life now more than ever! Suddenly I felt a warm heat go down both of my legs. I knew somehow it was a touch from the Lord.

That night, when a lot of people were sleeping in their hospital beds, in that long hallway as I walked...I asked the Lord to come back into my heart. I believe that night the Lord walked right along with me in that hospital hallway and just listened to me pouring out my heart to Him. He saw me crying, He knew I was hurting, and I believe He understood my pain. He didn't judge me or condemn me for how I felt. He loved me, and even when I had gotten angry at Him...He still loved me! He had not forgotten me, even if I had forgotten Him.

I told the Lord that I knew Michael was with Him now, and how much I missed my son! I said that I wanted to see him again, that I wanted to go to heaven. I told Him that I really didn't understand why this had happened to me and that I had so many questions. I also told Him not to have Michael's death be in vain...to somehow take the loss of my son and my pain and turn it all around, and one day let something good come from all of this. Those were just words from my heart that I was pouring out to the Lord, but I knew I meant them. That night I was changed in more than one way. There are just some things in life you never forget!

Chapter 26

I walked the whole floor several times that night. Each time around, I would move a little bit faster. I walked all night because I couldn't sleep? I was so full of energy, there was no way I could sit still. I watched as the sun came up the next morning and felt a freshness in the air I had never felt before. It was a new day to me, and I was a new person! I felt so full of life. For the first time in my life I felt good about myself, about who I was. I knew Steve and the girls were going to be coming anytime and I wanted to surprise them by meeting them at the elevator. So I waited by the elevator and looked out the window.

Then I spotted Steve and the girls walking into the hospital from the parking area. I thought my heart was going to explode as soon as I saw them, it started beating so fast. *That is my family,* I thought to myself. *I am truly blessed!* I stood by the elevator and waited for them to arrive on my floor. When the doors opened, Steve walked out with the girls, not expecting to see me standing there. I could tell by his face that he was shocked. His eyes filled with tears as soon as he saw me. He came toward me and gave me a kiss. Jessica ran right for me and Jennifer leaned toward me from Steve's arms for me to take her. I gladly put my arms out for Jennifer to come to me. It felt so good to hold my daughter!

We all walked back to my hospital room together as I began to tell Steve the whole story of what had happened to me. Steve had no choice but to believe me now, because I was standing right in front of him. I wonder what he must have felt that day when he walked off the elevator and saw me standing there? I never did truly ever ask him, because I was so in amazement at what had just happened to me. I still don't have all the answers to what truly happened to me that night. But I know one thing: I was healed! There are some spiritual things that happen in our lives that we do not understand. But that is all right, because one day we will. The most important thing is that I know I was touched by God that night!

Two days later I was released from the hospital. I still had no pain! The tests I had done when I checked into the hospital had showed that I had a large number of blood clots (DVT) in both my legs, two had penetrated my lungs, and one large one was in my femoral artery to my heart. But my recent tests had shown they had all vanished, except for the large one that was still in my femoral artery. But that clot was now 50% defaced. The doctor told me I would probably have that blood clot the rest of my life. Was he kidding me? He told me that if I would have a sudden jerk, the clot would probably move and kill me instantly.

I believed in my heart, though, that if God had healed me of the other blood clots, He would take care of this one too. The doctor kept saying that he could not get over the fact that the rest of my blood clots had all just vanished so quickly. But I was not surprised; I knew what had happened to me...I had been healed! My left leg was still pretty swollen, but little by little the swelling was going down. The doctor told me I just needed to stay off of it for a while—that if I had to go anywhere, to use a wheelchair. I was put on a strong dose of coumadin and told that I needed to have my blood checked every couple of days. I was also told that I could not get pregnant again—that if I did, I probably wouldn't survive.

Why would he say a thing like that to me? Had he forgotten that I had just buried my son? If I even thought about Michael, it was difficult just to breathe. The pain of losing my son was still very raw. I may have been healed in my body, but my heart was still in great pain. I knew somehow that I had to make it through the loss of my son, and with God's help I felt I could. Believe me, the last thing I was thinking about was having another child! All I wanted to do was go home and put all of this behind me. My prayers were finally answered, and I was able to go home!

The house felt different this time. It didn't seem to feel so empty. I still ached to hold my little baby and at times I missed him more than words can say. At times, my eyes would swell up with tears, and I could feel a lump forming in my throat when I would pick up one of the baby items to pack away. I felt I needed to pack up everything and get it out of the house. What was the sense of keeping the baby things around? Sometimes it was just too hard to see them day after day. Yes, I had my meltdowns, mostly when no one was around me. I had to be strong for Steve and the girls; they couldn't take seeing me cry. As weird as it sounds, there were times I could almost feel Michael with me. To this day, that part has never changed!

The hardest thing of all was visiting his grave. I'd wear my dark sunglasses so Steve and the girls wouldn't see me cry. Steve would always grab my hand and give it a squeeze while we stood there. It was his way of telling me, "We are in this together, and I am here for you!" Those things still happen to this day, twenty years later, every time we visit Michael's grave. I always lean down and pull any weeds that try to grow over Michael's flat stone. I feel like it's the least I can do. Then I place my hand on his stone and in my mind I tell him how much I love him and miss him.

Part of me knows he is not there, but it is still very hard to think of his little body in that cold ground. I can still feel the pain of our loss; it is something that just doesn't go away. There is nothing I can do to change what happened—my son is gone, and I can't bring him back. All I can do is pray, and that does help! I know in my heart where my son is and I know that one day I will go to heaven and see him again. I still do not understand why my son died or why I developed the blood clots I did. But for now, I take one day at a time in my life and try to live each and every day to the fullest! Because none of us know what can happen tomorrow.

Chapter 27

Looking back, I feel my life has been a journey. People say time heals all wounds...I guess that is kind of true. I believe that time helps you to come to terms with your loss. You never truly forget it, but time helps you to move on with your life. Through prayer and faith in the Lord, I have made it to where I am today. As I look back at all I have been through over the years, it feels like it was someone else who lived this life. But it wasn't someone else, it was actually me! I lived it, I walked it, I cried the tears, and I mourned the loss of our son. I survived only because of the Lord, and I am so thankful to Him!

Sometimes we forget where we have been and what we have been through. Writing this book has helped me to remember where I was, what I overcame, and where I am going. I believe every word in the Bible, and miracles are very real to me. I believe every time I stand, walk, or move my legs in any way, it's truly a miracle! I've come to realize that miracles still do happen—some are big and some are small. If you have ever had a miracle in your life or seen someone who has, then you know what I I'm talking about. No matter how seemingly big or small, they are all important!

God has been so good to me over the years! A few days after I got out of the hospital I started receiving cards and letters from people I had never met from all over the country. My mother-in-law later told me that a family member had run an ad for a card shower for me in *The Budget* (a local paper that is known locally, nationally, and internationally as the Amish newspaper).

At first it was hard for me to read the letters people wrote. But months and even years later, they helped me get through some of those really hard days. It helped so much to know that there were other people who knew just what I was feeling over the loss of our son.

A few weeks after I had left the hospital, I was up walking everywhere, and I felt great! It was almost as though it had all been just a dream. But deep down inside I knew that it wasn't. I decided one day to walk to get the mail. That day, we received a large envelope from the hospital addressed to me and Steve. I wondered what it could be and slowly opened it up. There inside that envelope were pictures of Michael the day he was born. I felt for a moment like I could not breathe and tried to gasp for air. Tears started streaming down my face and I could not stop them no matter how hard I tried. Everything that I had been through from the pregnancy to the birth of my son came flooding back to me.

The memories were both happy and sad. Happy, because I remembered how I felt when I was pregnant. Sad, because I remembered the pain I felt when I said good-bye to him. My heart ached now more than ever to hold my son. His pictures were not so pretty to look at because his skin had started to deteriorate. But to me, he was so beautiful! Steve was as deeply touched over the pictures as I was when I showed them to him. We now proudly display those same pictures with the rest of our family photos. We feel that even though he is not here with us, he is still very much a part of our family!

Later I came to find out that some hospitals take pictures of stillborn babies and mail them to the parents. It is a gift that some hospitals do weeks later for the parents free of charge. I cannot put into words how precious those pictures are to me! It is an amazing gift, and I am blessed every day just to have them. I now proudly show off all my children's pictures, including Michael's.

Many years later I had a dream that a nurse placed a little baby in my arms and leaned toward me and said, "This is your son." Then I heard a loud voice say, "You will have a son and name him James." I sat right up in bed in tears when I heard those words. I even woke Steve up and told him about the dream, but once again I think he thought I was nuts. That dream stayed with me; I couldn't stop thinking about it. A few months later, much to our surprise, I found out I was pregnant. That pregnancy, as well as the birth of my second son, is a whole other story in itself! In June 1994, I gave birth to a precious little boy, and of course we named him James.Through the pregnancy I developed five more blood clots, and I still had that blood clot in my femoral artery through it all. But no matter what I faced, I knew that the Lord would take care of me. He had healed me once and I knew He could do it again.

Oh, the stories I could tell! Like when several years ago I went with some friends to a Benny Hinn crusade in Florida. My friend's daughter was having some health issues and I was there to help support her. While Benny was praying on stage I felt heat go through my entire body. I opened my eyes and saw an angel standing right in front of me. The angel said, "You are healed. You have no more blood clots anywhere, even the large one in the femoral artery is gone!" I closed my eyes and started crying, and when I opened my eyes the angel was gone.

Was it a dream or a vision? I really can't answer that, I just know I felt a sudden urge to go forward toward the stage. A man came up to me and asked what had happened to me, and I began to tell him. The next thing I knew, he took me by the hand and we passed a line of people. He took me right up to the platform to Pastor Benny, who then prayed over me, and the power of God went all the way through me again. I still questioned what had happened to me, and if I was really healed. It was not until months later while at home when I became very ill with migraine headaches and had to go to the hospital.

There they did several tests on me, one of which was blood work. Later a nurse came into my room and told me that my blood work was normal and showed that I had no blood clots anywhere in my body. I guess that was when it truly hit me that I was totally healed. The blood clot that was in my femoral artery for over fifteen years was finally gone, as well as the others! God had actually healed me! I am proud to tell you that today I have no blood clots anywhere in my body and I take no medications to prevent them...I AM TOTALLY HEALED!

I have been in ministry now for over fifteen years. I have spoken at many churches, and to this day God still amazes me! Years ago I asked God to turn around what I had been through... to let something good come from it. I believe He is doing just that! When the Lord put it in my heart to write this book, I knew it would be an emotional journey for me. I have cried over many of these pages as I was writing them. Yes, I still clearly remember what I felt back then. But something else happened to me while writing this book—I found peace and understanding.

I have been blessed witnessing to others about my story. I have seen people find hope once again in their lives. I don't know what you might be facing and I don't know what you have been through...everyone has a story. But I do know someone who can help you: His name is Jesus. He knows right where you are, what you are going through, and He will listen to you when it seems like no one else will. He will not judge you or condemn you. Believe it or not, He really loves you!

Yes, I believe I gave birth to an angel, because I believe that children are little angels sent to us from up above. Some of our little angels have passed on, but they will always be in our hearts and a part of our lives. No matter how old you get, you will always remember them. So please don't judge me if I call my son a little angel, because the words come from a mother's heart. To me...my son Michael will always be an angel. My question to you is: Do you now believe in little angels?

Afterword:

Many people sent me cards, letters, and encouraging words during my time of my loss. A lot of these people I don't even know, yet they took the time to write me. I would like to share some of these writings with you. I pray they can bring you as much strength in your everyday life as they have in my mine. Below is a copy of the ad that was run in *The Budget* for me.

April 11, 1990

My heart aches for you so, since hearing of your battle with phlebitis. One of Steve's cousins attended our church and told me about all you have been through. I called Steve's mom this morning and she gave me an 800 number to call you. I tried twice but got a recording saying the number dialed is incorrect, so I decided to just write you a quick line.

One of your daughters answered the phone and she sounded so cute! I thank the Lord that the girls are where I am sure they are well cared for and you needn't worry. A group of our church ladies have a prayer chain and we prayed for you this morning. We trust the Lord will send healing out to you through proper medication ministered to you. It can't be easy to be bedfast after a difficult pregnancy and having given birth to a little angel that is now in Heaven.

Were it not for the precious promise that the Lord will not allow anything in our lives but what He sees us through, we'd give up in despair at such times. We have a Amish lady in our area who also was hospitalized a week or so after giving birth to a baby. It's taking some time for the phlebitis to dissolve and heal up.

It undoubtedly pays to obey doctor's orders, to really take it easy for a while even after you leave the hospital. Here's wishing you and Steve a Happy Easter even if you have it in the hospital. We'll continue remembering you both in our prayers.

"The Lord will guide you always, He will satisfy your needs, in a sun scorched land and will strengthen your frame, you will be a whole watered garden, like a spring whose waters never fail."

Isa. 58:11
Sincerely In Christ,
Mary

Hello

Just a few lines your way this rainy Tues. PM. Hope be now you are no longer in the hospital, but recovering rapidly at home! When I saw your name in the Budget, I thought to myself "I just have to write to this lady." You see, it is little more than a year since I was in the hospital for 10 days. I had a blood clot above the knee. Up till then I had spent about 6 weeks in bed with a bad right leg.

I got phlebitis from the knee up, and when that was about gone, I got the clot in my left leg. In the deep veins of course and ended up in the hospital. My experience was a little different though; I wasn't quite 2 months pregnant. So I was very upset to be put on blood thinner. Dr. said it was a very complicated situation, being on blood thinner and being pregnant. I had to learn to give myself shots of heprin (blood thinner).

For me that was a very hard thing to do! I used these shots for 9 months. We thank God that we have a little boy by the name of Nathan. He seems all-normal, except for a double thumb on one hand, but it's down to the first joint only. Also he has a soft spot in the windpipe which sometimes collapses when he inhales. Which makes it hard to breathe at times and makes a strange sound. He has more problems with respiratory problems.

But enough of that, I am writing you a letter to cheer you up, not to write about me. If you have time and want to, I would enjoy hearing from you sometime. I wonder if you have any other children, if so what are their names, ages? I wonder if you have spent lots of time in bed before, or just since now.

May God be with you through all your trials. He knows what is best for us and someday we will understand. Things sure looked dark for us at times, but He saw us through! Keep looking up! Never loose faith in Him! He careth for you!

Praying for you,
Amos & Irene

April 11, 1990

Dear Unknown friends,

Greetings of love in Jesus Holy Name. Wonder how you are by now? I just saw your name in the Budget and wanted to write. Yesterday was dreap-n-cool had some rain again, now cooled off and feels like snow today. I have some tomatoes, cabbage outside. My radishes and lettuce aren't up yet. John plowed the garden Saturday, but now it's wet again! But I am sure it will dry out again soon.

School is out here, but our oldest is in first grade. He wasn't quite through reading, so I am helping him. Which isn't too easy with three other children trying to write and color on the same table. But they are happy to be apart of it.

John works as a carpenter most days, but isn't today, as it is too cold! We also have 9 cows, 30 sows, sell feeder pigs and have 600 pullets for hatchery eggs, and 170 ducks for hatchery too. So we have plenty to do. See youns had a still-born-Sometimes you wonder how things can go like that, but there's nothing promised! Feel kinda shaky, as it you never know what will happen.

I'm due any day with our 5th one. We already have 2 boys and 2 girls, they are all healthy! Which we can't be thankful enough for. I have had 4 c-sections now but since have changed doctors. We are hoping to have this one normal. Guess time will tell. The good Lord knows best!

Well maybe you don't feel like reading. I must go get dinner started and I have more eggs to case and wash. We are always glad for letters to, if you feel like writing. But we do understand, not everyone can get a letter back. So take care of yourself. Let us keep each other in prayer.

Love-n-Prayers,
John & Laura

April 12. 1990

Dear Friends,

Greetings of love in our dear Savior's name. Although we are strangers, I think we have something in common as we too lost our baby almost 5 months now. He was stillborn, too. I hope you are recovering again! I had a c-section, so I had to take extra care too.

At the time I didn't really think this was something I'd get over, but with time and God's help things began to look brighter again! My husband and I talked about it and we decided it's like a wound. It heals over and the hurt goes away, but there is still a scar (the memories)!

Hopefully we were strengthened in our spiritual life by it too. We know that everything works together for good tot hem that love God, to them that are called according to His purpose.

Romans 8:28
We will close wishing you God's blessings in your life,
Mr. & Mrs. Yoder

Debbie,

I am sorry this has happened to you. I did not feel Jacob kicking for 3-4 days. I called the doctor and He told us that it didn't look good & sent us to Union for an ultrasound. As we expected, we lost our baby. They induced my labor April 26th and I had Jacob at 1:07am on the 27th. He was a beautiful boy-even at 6 months. The funeral was on the 30th.

    We were very fortunate that we had our family, friends, preacher & doctor behind me. It helped in this terrible time. We still hurt! The worst time for me was at night when it was very quite. I would have a lot of time to think and it made it hard to go to sleep. We know that we have to move on, Jacob will be with us always. It helps to know that there are others out there whose hearts are aching also.

    Amy

In Loving Memory Of
Our Son
Michael Steven Miller